MAN of GRACE

A Remembrance of
Paul Wells Barrus

By Mary Cimarolli

Mary Cimarolli

Published by
TEXAS A&M UNIVERSITY-COMMERCE

First Edition
ISBN 978-1-4507-0639-1
Printed in the United States of America

Library of Congress Cataloging-in-Publication Data

Cimarolli, Mary, 1931–

Man of Grace
A Remembrance of Paul Wells Barrus

Includes sources

1. Barrus, Paul Wells, 1902 – 2000 — Academic —
20th century — Biography — Teaching —
Catholic Priest — East Texas — Winterset, Iowa

Design and production by
Hannah Blakely Barton

For all the great teachers in the world
and for all those who have been inspired
by at least one great teacher

PERSONAE

In the course of a life that spans almost one hundred years, names change—manners of address change—relationships change. I have attempted to keep the nomenclature used in this text in proper sequence. If I have fallen short in places, I offer the following explanatory note.

Paul Wells Barrus was known as Mr. Barrus to his Iowa students from 1919 to 1943. For a relatively short, though memorable, time, 1943 to 1945, he was known as Private Barrus. From 1949 when he received his Ph.D. degree and moved to Texas, he was Dr. Barrus. In 1978, upon his ordination to the priesthood, he became Father Barrus, or to those who knew him well, Father Paul. To family members, he was always known as "Cuz," and to his friends down through the years, he was Paul.

Even "Paul" could become a confusing name in this story because Father Paul Barrus served as assistant pastor at St. Paul the Apostle Catholic Church, and he shared first names with his good friend and caregiver, Paul Reittinger, who in the course of this story becomes Deacon Paul Reittinger.

Most confusing might be the changing names of Paul Barrus' beloved Texas college where he taught for so many years. Known as East Texas State Normal College from 1917 to 1923, it became East Texas State Teachers College in 1923, and East Texas State College in 1957. In 1965, it became East Texas State University and was renamed in 1996 as Texas A&M University-Commerce. Known by seven names in its one hundred-plus years, it will long be known as ET, and it is ET that I have chosen to use throughout the text when to do otherwise might be more confusing.

ACKNOWLEDGMENTS

When Paul Barrus was about to compliment someone to a great degree, perhaps even an excessive degree, say, for example, a hostess who had prepared for him an elaborate meal, he was known to preface his compliments with these words, "Now I don't intend to be fulsome, but…"

As I begin my acknowledgments, I don't intend to be fulsome, but… this book would never have become a reality had I not been given access to the personal interviews with Paul Barrus that friends and colleagues had the foresight to conduct, nor without the thousands of words he himself wrote about his life, ideas, experiences, and observations, and most certainly not without the interviews granted to me by his friends and associates in both of his professional lives—that of an educator par excellence and that of a Roman Catholic Priest extraordinaire.

It is to Father Henry that I owe the most gratitude. (He is now a monsignor, and although many in the clergy wear the title proudly, Henry Petter, a personable, gentle, unassuming man, encourages his long-time parishioners to call him "Father.") The day I declared to Father Henry, "I'm ready to begin work on Father Paul's story," he handed me my old professor's briefcase stuffed with his personal papers, letters, scrapbooks, poems, and phone messages scratched on little pieces of paper; notes on conversations they had shared; newspaper clippings of Barrus interviews; clippings of news stories written by others which Barrus had enjoyed and/or commented on; short stories and homilies Barrus himself had written; and even notes on his first retreats. Also, he gave me photo albums filled with highlights of Barrus' life as a priest, and congratulatory letters from friends on the occasions of his priestly anniversaries. Perhaps most delightful of all are the letters he had kept from students in his very first classes who had written to him with fond remembrances when they, too, were old. In addition, Father Henry found time in his busy life to talk to me at length about his good friend, to locate people I might interview, to give me phone numbers and addresses I might need, to encourage me every way he could, every step of the way.

And to Deacon Paul Reittinger who, along with Father Henry, gave Paul Barrus a chance to live a dignified old age by becoming his caregiver, albeit with a difference, many owe a debt of gratitude. When his body failed to keep up with his mind and spirit, they kept him going. They are the reasons he was able to be a productive, useful human being to the end.

Dr. James Conrad of Texas A&M University-Commerce gave me complete access to the Paul Barrus archives in the Special Collections housed in the Gee Library there. In addition, he offered personal advice, made photographs available to me, and was helpful in more ways than I can ever express.

To Dr. Frances Neidhardt, Judith Rudoff, Corrine Crow, and Nanci Carroll, all of whom conducted at-length personal interviews with Barrus, I owe heartfelt thanks, and say to each of them: thank you for having the foresight I did not have to interview Dr. Barrus, for recording those interviews so meticulously, and for making them available for others to use.

Until I drove to Baylor University, where he teaches, to interview him, I knew Dr. Ralph Wood only by reputation: outstanding former ET student and good friend of Paul Barrus, a man with a Ph.D. degree in religion and literature from the University of Chicago, a former Wake Forest University professor, a highly respected writer and scholar. As we shook hands that day, all my feelings of inadequacy as a writer surfaced in the presence of someone I felt was much better-qualified and much better suited for the particular task I had carved out for myself. Dr. Wood could not have been more gracious nor encouraging. He urged me to continue, and he promised to be my first reader/critic. His enthusiasm for this book, from beginning to end, has been for me the light that did not dim.

And, finally, how can one properly thank the late Linck family of Commerce: Dr. Charles and Dr. Ernestine, for collecting certain of the Paul Barrus "A Moment of Grace" columns from *The Commerce Journal*, and re-publishing them in *Moments of Grace*. This small book spared me many hours of research time in the archives of the local newspaper. Dr. Linck also had insightful and often humorous anecdotes about his professional and personal association with Dr. Barrus. Long after our "formal" interview, he continued to regale me with perceptive fragments of information via e-mail. (Charles Linck was very much alive as I began this book several years ago, and his often expressed wish was that it would be published before he died.)

Dr. Fred Tarpley was most generous with his time, granting me the whole of one cold, rainy afternoon in March of 2006 when I first began work on this book, to talk about his friend of many years. Fred Tarpley was a sophomore student when Paul Barrus came to ET. Through the years, they became fast friends, each having served, in turn, as department head. Dr. Tarpley has stayed with me from the beginning through the final editing of this book in February, 2010, and I am deeply indebted to him, my mentor.

Dr. Carroll Adams spoke graciously of his long-time friend and colleague, Paul Barrus, answered all of my questions, and gave me particular insight into Barrus' long struggle with depression, and the late Dr. Lawrence McNamee was kind enough to grant me an interview toward the end of his life. A light came into his eyes when he described in a weakened voice the many times he and Paul Barrus had performed an act they called "Barroom Ballads" for the English Department faculty at small gatherings and for the student body at "Faculty Frolics." Dr. James Byrd, although already deceased at the time of my interview with his ET colleagues, was also helpful because he had left wonderful written recollections of the relationship he shared with Dr. Barrus. And Dr. Byrd's niece, Annette Milton, contributed her store of Barrus memories.

Theresa Petter, Father Henry's sister-in-law, relived her memories of Father Paul in vivid writing via e-mail when we could not arrange a face-to-face interview for this work. Father Paul was already a priest, serving at St. Joseph Catholic Church in Commerce, when she enrolled as a student in the university. Never his student in a classroom, Theresa came to know him through their association in the Newman

Club at St. Joseph Parish, and she would be the first to say she never stopped learning from him during their long friendship.

Two relatives of Paul Barrus also came to my assistance: Elizabeth Johnson and Mary Jane Maiers, daughters of his beloved first cousin, Betty, with whom he was raised and who is now deceased. Their wonderful stories of "Cuz," lend a touch of humor to his story and reveal a side of his personality not seen by all those who knew him. I am particularly indebted to Mary Jane (now known as Jane) who did a masterful job in sorting through the hundreds of letters and for helping me select those which we felt would be most representative of Paul Barrus as a letter writer extraordinaire.

Time has not dimmed the memory nor the affection of one of Father Paul's devoted caretakers, Maria Rudnik, who attended Father Paul at the end of his life. Maria granted me a long interview, for which I am most grateful.

I must not neglect to mention others who helped in various important ways: Dr. Salvatore Attardo who came to my rescue when I had despaired of finding a publisher; Dr. Gary Peer, Interim Provost and Vice President of Academic Affairs, who helped to obtain a grant from Texas A&M-Commerce; Dr. Hunter Hayes, Editor, *Sam Rayburn Series on Rural Life*; and of course, my editors: Dr. Fred Tarpley, Mr. Bill Anderson, and Texas A&M-Commerce student, Hector Guiterrez. Karen Wood, Linda Banks, Marilyn Stacey, and Susan Garza were all willing and careful readers.

And last, but most important to me, has been the advice, constant reassurance, support, and love of my husband, John S. Robottom, from the beginning of this labor of love to its end.

If I have inadvertently omitted the names of some who were helpful to me, I beg forgiveness.

CONTENTS

PREFACE

Grow old along with me!
The best is yet to be,
The last of life, for which the first was made:
Our times are in His hand
Who saith, "A whole I planned,
Youth shows but half; trust God: See all nor be afraid!"

—Robert Browning
Rabbi Ben Ezra (1864)

THIS ACCOUNT OF PAUL WELLS BARRUS, the boy, the adolescent, and the adult professional, begins as a recollection of a life well-lived and appreciated by many who still live. His story spans the 20th century, minus two and one half years—through the administrations of two Roosevelts and two Bushes, to say nothing of King Edward VII, Kaiser Wilhelm II, and the welcome demise of the Thousand-year Reich and the Soviet Union. Add to that some echoes of "Grey's Elegy in a Country Churchyard."

His life, however, was not one of grandeur but one of service, humble though remarkably well documented by him and by many others who loved and valued him as teacher, counselor, and toward the end of his life, as effective and well-regarded Roman Catholic priest.

The early parts of this book describe his life in a small Midwestern town and his early and surprisingly rigorous high school curriculum, which formed his later academic success and commitment to learning. These chapters further describe the distinguished academic and teacher at East Texas State University for thirty years; a man who came to teach and left as legend.

Later chapters describe a committed Catholic who belatedly and improbably became a Roman Catholic priest, and how, toward the end of his long, productive life, two remarkable men became his loving brothers in Christ, caregivers to a degree unimaginable to those who did not witness it. He died in the presence of those who truly cherished him and was buried beside his mother in Winterset, Iowa, by the friends who had sustained him in late-life.

In the life story of Paul Barrus, there may be wisdom to be found in the Eastern European legend, possibly of Hasidic origin, that thirty-two righteous men sustain the moral universe. If this number drops below thirty-two, the legend goes, the moral universe is certain to collapse. Although no longer here to shoulder his portion of that universe, we need not worry about its imminent collapse because Paul Wells Barrus, for one, touched so many lives and inspired so many people to rise above their ordinariness, and to become, each in turn, supporting shoulders.

This man exemplified learning, holiness, decency—indeed every happy gift. He had a life that encompassed the three dimensions of Newtonian cosmology, and yet the profound remembrances of hundreds of people he touched make us believe he also had a transcendental dimension. When we say we are richer for having known him, it may be because he has given us insight into an unexpected level of perception—a glimpse into a world we must visit while there is yet time.

His intrinsic qualities overshadowed his physical characteristics. He was of average height and weight, had dark hair before it turned gray, and deep blue eyes which twinkled behind horn-rimmed glasses. In the classroom, he had a serious demeanor, but a little smile would move almost imperceptibly across his face when he was amused. He laughed heartily with friends and colleagues. He never called attention to himself, but people gravitated toward him. Formal in speech and manner, always correct, he could be intimidating to those uneasy with their command of language, but to all who knew him well, he was gentle, self-assured, and charismatic in his own quiet way. He seems to have met every major crisis in his life with personal, as well as divine, grace.

Although he left behind beautiful journals and personal letters, an outstanding Master of Arts degree thesis and a distinguished Doctor of Philosophy dissertation, this gifted and prolific writer, a man of true belles lettres, published very little for the general public or the academic community outside of newspaper columns and a few monographs. How is such a man to be remembered long after those who now live are gone? How does one presume to write about a larger-than-life figure — indeed, how does one breathe life into a legend?

This man touched my life in such a way that he became part of it after I returned to college at age thirty-eight although there was a period of about fifteen years in a thirty-year acquaintance when I was only vaguely aware of where he was and what he was doing. In the usual sense, I cannot say he was a constant presence in my life; rather, his influence was an indelible presence. In particular, I was very fortunate he came back into my life at one of its lowest ebbs, a time when I was most in need of assurance and guidance. From that time on, I did not lose touch with him again until his death.

In some instances, I have drawn on memories of my long acquaintance with my former professor who later, rather improbably, became my parish priest. When I was his student, I was aware that he was a Roman Catholic, but I did not know that he was a convert to the Faith as I was. It was just before his death that I realized we had had that in common all along.

This is not a biography, and I have every hope it will not be regarded as hagiography. It is rather a recollection and remembrance. I have drawn heavily from the recollections of his friends and family and from personal interviews which others have recorded. Sometimes I quote from my class notes without apology and make reference to his impact on my life when it chanced to cross paths with his. In the course of writing this appreciation of Paul Barrus, I realized, on reviewing what I had written, that I had used verbatim much of his own writing and comments. My narrative seemed nothing more than a filigree to bind his quotations into a stately procession.

Belatedly, I recalled that James Boswell had done precisely this in his incomparable life of Samuel Johnson. As Johnson himself remarked and Boswell duly recorded: "Depend upon it, Sir: When a man knows he is to be hanged in a fortnight, it composes his mind wonderfully!" No commentary of Boswell's could have captured Johnson's own voice. Wisely, he did not try. My filigree may do little more than move this story along; I make no apology for following so distinguished a predecessor.

MAN *of* GRACE

A Remembrance of
Paul Wells Barrus

By Mary Cimarolli

PART I

A MAN FROM WINTERSET

Good-bye to a Good Life in Commerce

MORNING OF A SUMMER DAY, 1979: an old man with his suitcase beside him and two remarkably successful careers behind him stands alone near the railroad tracks leading out of Commerce, Texas, a town of 7,000, sixty-five miles northeast of Dallas, home of East Texas State Teachers College with an enrollment of 2,400 when, as a newly hired professor, he had arrived here on a cold winter evening in 1949. Now, shielding his eyes from the bright August sun, he tries to picture Commerce as it had looked from that same spot the day he had stepped off the train thirty years before to sit alone, waiting, on the platform bench of The Cotton Belt Railroad station.

True, there was no longer a platform or passenger service from Commerce, and it would be his cousin, Betty, who would drive him to his destination in Des Moines, Iowa, but this was as close as he could get to re-creating that moment when he had arrived alone in this little town he had come to love in spite of its many differences from his native Winterset, Iowa.

In his own words, Paul Barrus left this account of his memorable arrival in Commerce, January, 1949, during

> . . . one of the worst ice storms in the town's history.
> Coming from Iowa, I had looked forward to the

"Sunny South." No one met me at the station and
it was pitch dark. A young man standing nearby offered me a ride "uptown" in his pickup. Passing the
old Acker Hotel, I observed that I might stay there.
"Oh you wouldn't want to stay there," he said rather
grimly. "I'll take you up to Mrs. Yarbrough's. She
has a room made vacant today." Fannie Yarbrough,
on Ash Street, took me in for the night and I stayed
19 months.[6]

The next morning, a Sunday, he set out to look over the campus of
East Texas State Teachers College. A rather bleak image awaited him
as he trudged through the ice and snow:

The sky was like lead, a chilly wind was blowing,
and the between-semester break had emptied the
college of students. The spring semester began the
next morning. I was assigned to teach two classes
in freshman English, two sections of sophomore
literature (from Beowulf to Wordsworth and from
Wordsworth to the present), and a class in the history of the English language.

As he walked around the campus that first day, he must have
thought of Drake University where he had been elected to Phi Beta
Kappa and from which he had received his bachelor's and master's
degrees, and of the University of Iowa from which he had recently
graduated with a Ph.D. degree. On both of those campuses, as well
as Iowa State where he had also taught, there were always a few stray
students about during semester break; usually those who lived too
far away to go home, but here, there was no snowball throwing, no
laughter, no students. Later that day at the local Catholic Church,
he found that there were only eight parishioners present at the once-
a-week Mass. No more daily Mass for me, he must have thought as
he walked around the deserted campus, remembering that his Iowa
friends had been apprehensive about his intention to teach in Texas,
telling him, "They don't like Catholics in the South! You'll have a
hard time." Fortunately, their predictions never came true, as Barrus
himself has said:

… for I never suffered the slightest embarrassment because of my religious faith. There were some humorous incidents, however, when I met my first classes. At the end of a session with Shakespeare, one girl gathered up her books and in a stage whisper remarked to her companion, "Well, he may be a Catholic, but he seems to know what he's talking about!" The next day, word spread quickly that there was a new Catholic in town. Overheard at the barber shop was this tidbit: "And he's been hired to teach out at the college! What are things coming to? To get a job out to the college these days, looks as though you have to be a Yankee and a Catholic."[2]

As it turned out, this seems to be a rather premature worry on the part of this barbershop philosopher. It does reflect, however, the feeling some locals appeared to have that the college was beginning to take on some pretensions, and although he may not have "suffered embarrassment" because of his religious faith, as he expressed it, he seems not to have spoken openly of his conversion to Catholicism. I think he was well aware that Catholic converts are often suspected of trying to convert others, and he did not want to encourage such an erroneous assumption about his own belief.

This first week, he took great delight in the conversation of his new office mates who introduced him to Texas expressions. "Here comes that student who just *warts* me to death," one said. Barrus looked at her hands but could see no warts. The Texas version of the word sorry also surprised him. "Up home, the word *sorry* carried only connotations of regret, but now it proved to be a term of infinite variety and matchless shades of meaning. There are no substitutes for 'She's a *sorry* housekeeper' and 'He's just plumb *sorry*.'"

Throughout his years at ET, he was a bit of an anomaly on campus. His former student, Dr. Ralph Wood, says of this awareness: "He knew that he was odd, but then he also knew that we are all a bit strange, and that God himself is the oddest of all. I think that Dr. Barrus enjoyed being eccentric if only because, as a Latinist, he knew that the word literally means 'off-center'."

As one might expect, that first week must have been difficult, but he was soon smitten with the place, as he expressed it much later on April 24, 1995, in a faculty address on Paul Barrus Day: "I came to remain two years and stayed on the faculty for twenty-seven."

His friends — those he had taught and those he had taught with over the years at East Texas State University, those parishioners he had counseled as both deacon and priest at the small Catholic Church in Commerce after retirement from his long teaching career, and friends from all walks of life had gathered a few days before he left to wish him a safe trip back to Iowa. The farewell had been warm and genuine. He had felt the love of those he had known for many years, and yet a sadness could be read in the faces of those who gathered that evening — so deeply etched into the evening itself — that all the good wishes washing over him could not wish it away. He would be missed. He, who had received highest accolades from this small town where he had taught for so many years, and who, after retirement from college teaching had remained in Commerce to begin another life would, in all likelihood, they feared, soon be blind.

Contemplation of the long, sad journey back to Iowa on that day in 1979 with which this book begins gave him plenty of time to think — not only about his early years at ET, nor about his later ecclesiastical life, but about his future as well. He remembered the great laugh he had shared with his friends over F. Scott Fitzgerald's famous line about there being no second acts in American lives when at the age of 74 he was ordained as a permanent deacon in the Dallas Diocese. Barrus has said that he walked out of St. Joseph's in Commerce one morning while he was still teaching at ET and noticed some pamphlets in the foyer of the church describing a course of study which would train deacons for the diocese. He knew immediately that was what he wanted to do. He enrolled in the next course to be offered and completed the full cycle of study. A member of St. Joseph parish since moving to Commerce, he served as permanent deacon there from 1974–1978. A permanent deacon has many duties similar to those of a priest. He may baptize, assist at Mass, give homilies, offer instruction in the faith, and assist at funerals, along with other assigned duties.

In 1976, midway into his four-year service as a deacon, he met the young, recently ordained Henry Vincent Petter, then serving as assistant pastor at the Immaculate Conception Catholic Church in

Tyler, at a monthly gathering for East Texas priests and deacons. It was customary for this group to break into pairs to walk what they called "The Emmaus Way" together. This reference to the Emmaus Way comes from Chapter 24, verses 13–15 of St. Luke's Gospel in The King James Version of the Holy Bible: *"And behold, two of them went that same day to a village called Emmaus, which was from Jerusalem about threescore furlongs. And they talked together of all these things which had happened. And it came to pass, that, while they communed together and reasoned, Jesus himself drew near, and went with them."* As Deacon Paul Barrus and Father Henry Petter walked the Emmaus Way together that day, Barrus has said he was impressed by the modesty and grace of the younger man, sensing immediately that he would like to know this priest better. That chance came a few months later when the group met at St. Joseph's in Commerce, and the two once again walked the Emmaus Way together. Father Henry recounts his early impression of Deacon Paul Barrus:

> I was surprised to learn that he was not married. I noticed his command of the English language right away. Every word he spoke registered perfectly. I saw him as a holy and reflective kind of person; as a learned man. I don't recall his having mentioned then that he was a convert. He seemed to be a person who gave an enormous amount of love to whatever he was doing. I began to see the lighter side of him as we walked around the ET campus. I noticed that he was having trouble with his eyesight, and I picked up on his fear of not being useful as he was aging."[13]

Ordinarily, a permanent deacon never becomes a priest. In the case of Deacon Paul Barrus, church officials took notice of this most unusual man. As Father Paul later reported, "Msgr. Robert Rehkemper, vicar general of the diocese, asked me if I were interested in becoming a priest. I told him it was my lifelong dream." Word of his wish became known to Bishop Tschoepe of the Dallas Diocese, who decided to take his request for ordination to the Sacred Congregation of Clergy when he went to Rome in 1978. The petition included a request that he be excused from attending seminary because of his age, the history of his studies, and the extraordinary knowledge he already possessed.

During his college days, Barrus had taken nearly every course he would have needed had he entered the seminary then.

Permission was granted, provided that Deacon Barrus could pass the required examination. His fellow professor at ET, Dr. Fred Tarpley, says of the proposed examination, "The English department at ET had great fun with that caveat because they all remembered the story of the great Chaucer scholar, George Lyman Kittredge at Harvard, who, when someone asked when he would get his doctorate, replied, 'Now, who would examine me?' Of course Dr. Barrus, unlike Kittredge, was not pompous, but upon hearing that he would have to take an examination, the English Department people all said, "But who would examine Dr. Barrus?"

And so it came to pass some two years later. Paul Barrus was ordained a Roman Catholic priest at St. William Catholic Church in Greenville, Texas, on December 16, 1978, when he was seventy-six years old: he was a priest at last, "a priest forever, according to the order of Melchizedek." (Hebrews 5:6)

The ordination was moved from St. Joseph to the larger Greenville location to accommodate all those, Catholic and non-Catholic, who wanted to attend this special occasion for which their special friend, Paul Barrus, had waited so long. Dr. Tarpley, who had attended the ordination, recalled that Bishop Tschoepe told the assembled congregation at one point: "I am supposed to say, 'My Son,' at this time, but in this case, I will say, 'My Brother.'" Those at the ordination were greatly amused at Bishop Tschoepe's remark about the change of wording from "son" to "brother". Everyone present was well-aware of the unusual nature of ordaining a man of advanced age. It was a great tribute to Barrus who had proven that, although he was old, he still had much to offer.

With what joy he must have begun his new life as a priest at his home parish in Commerce. After all, how many of us are given the chance to do it all over again at the age of seventy-six? Already familiar with this parish and its parishioners, he began his priestly life in anticipation of serving there for the remainder of his life. For about two years, all went well. He said Holy Mass, performed his routine sacramental duties, and drove his own car. Both he and the people he served were satisfied in their relationship with each other, but disappointment was waiting. He had long lived in fear of going blind. Now, his vision problems were worsening steadily. He was forced to have eye surgery. It went badly, and his vision deteriorated rapidly. For a relatively short time, he had been able to live his lifelong dream of being a priest. It appeared as if his Second Act had come to an untimely end—a dark end.

One can only imagine the despondency with which he returned to Iowa. Trying hard to fight back the depression he knew well, he vowed to make the best of his new situation. He would be as much help as he possibly could for as long as he could to the Sisters of Mercy who were in charge of the retirement home where he would live in Des Moines.

Hello to the Retirement Home and The Sisters of Mercy in Des Moines

At long last, back in Iowa, but not to his beloved hometown of Winterset, he set about trying to make the best of a bad situation. Once settled in, he regained his passion for life because he soon saw there was much to do, and he still had much to offer. The Sisters delighted in his presence and were grateful for the help he gave them. He counseled residents of the Home, heard confessions, and offered The Holy Sacrifice of the Mass at every opportunity. He became, and remained for many years, good friends with some of the Sisters. And of course, as long as he could see well enough to write, he continued his long-standing practice of writing letters every day. In addition, he was a careful and sympathetic listener to residents of the home. He was curious about where they had come from, and he genuinely wanted to know their stories. Sometimes they needed someone to listen to them more than they needed medicine or medical attention. He was fascinated with their idiosyncrasies, their sense of place, and now, their sense of displacement. He never forgot their stories, and in later years he wrote a few short stories based on what they had told him.

Now in Des Moines, so close to Winterset, he often visited his home town, and he probably spent a great deal of time at this point in his life remembering that place he once described this way: "I sometimes feel twinges of nostalgia for the scarlet sumac, the brilliant hard maples, and the misty-gold October afternoons. Although Texas and Texans have been good to me, when I think of Winterset, I think of home."[11]

How can we hope to understand this person who was, all of his life, so distinctly, "a man from Winterset" without understanding those early forces which shaped him? Sense of place was always extremely important to him. He loved to repeat a story the Georgia writer Flannery O'Connor once told about visiting with a group of writers at a conference in New York City. When asked if she had enjoyed the group, she replied, "Oh, they were interesting, but the trouble is *they ain't from nowhere.*" No one could ever say of Paul Barrus, or Flannery O'Connor: "*They ain't from nowhere.*"

Recollections About Early Life in Winterset

He was born there in 1902, but the heart of his story begins with the untimely death of his mother when he was seven years old. In his own words, Paul Barrus left the following account of her traumatic death:

> I remember the last day before my mother died. It was a Sunday, the Fourth of July, and I had just turned seven in June; my baby brother, Dale, was two months old. We were at my grandparents' house for a family celebration of my cousin Joe's recent recovery from brain fever. We had just finished a bountiful dinner, and I was playing marbles on the floor with my cousin, my age, when I suddenly had the urge to sit in my mother's lap. She said, "Paul, you're getting too old to sit in my lap." I said, "It's because I love you, Mother."
>
> My playmate went home to spend the night with me. He and I wanted to pop firecrackers, but because it was a Sunday, Mother took them from us and put them on a top shelf, promising: "We will fire them first thing tomorrow morning."
>
> It was that same night she died from a blood clot in her leg. She was twenty-seven years old, and it was in the middle of the night. My cousin and I were asleep in my bed at the end of a long, long room. My parents and my baby brother were asleep at the other end of the room. I was awakened by my brother's crying. My father said something to wake

Paul's Mother, Daisy

my mother, but she never stirred. It was during one of those summer storms with lightning and rain. My father crawled out of the window and ran to the neighbor's house for help. Soon the room was filled with people. My grandmother was chafing my mother's arms and wrists, trying to bring her back to life. I remember lying in bed praying, "Dear God, don't let my mother die." But I knew instinctively that she would. *My beautiful Irish mother with jet black hair and dark blue eyes.* Her name was Daisy. It was 1909.[13]

On the day of my mother's funeral, the pastor took for his text these words, "Her sun has gone down while yet it is day." I was held up so I could take a last look at my mother as she lay in her casket. I took one brief look, and looked away. . . . And so every year, for me the Fourth of July is a reenactment of

9

my mother's sudden death. The firecrackers were
never fired, and for years afterwards, I could not
celebrate the Fourth because it was the anniversary
of her death.[12]

None of Paul Barrus' second cousins, or the widow of his first cousin,
Hugh (all interviewed for this story) know exactly why his English
father, C. A. Barrus, chose the infant, Dale, to rear after his young
wife's death, but left seven-year-old Paul to the care of Daisy's family.
It has always been the belief of his cousins that Daisy Barrus had, on
her deathbed, asked her mother, Mary Wells Clopton, and Mary's
sister Cora, to raise Paul. The factual basis for this belief seems shaky,
however, because according to Barrus' own account of her death, the
blood clot passing from her leg through her heart would have caused
instant death. It seems entirely possible that he could have read this
request of his mother to her mother and sister back into his life story,
since he was concerned always to idealize his mother. It seems equally
possible the request could have been made before this time for reasons
that were never fully explained to him nor his cousins.

In his later years, Barrus told of the time when, shortly after his
mother's death, he had stopped by a Catholic church one day while
on an errand for his grandmother. He had looked up at the altar
and had seen the statue of a beautiful woman holding a baby. A sudden feeling of peace had come over him—a feeling of warmth and
beauty—a sense of belonging. It was as if, he said, he had seen his
deceased mother holding his baby brother, Dale. He knew at that moment that he wanted to become a Catholic, but his grandparents and
other relatives who were in charge of his upbringing were Protestant.
He said that he had held on to the memory of this epiphany for more
than thirty years before he actually converted to Catholicism.[13]

The boy had free access to both houses, and he grew up with his
Aunt Cora's four children: two boys and two girls. Cora's son, Hugh,
only four months younger than Paul, was his favorite playmate. Aunt
Cora treated him like a son, and whatever toy or treat she purchased
for her own son, she also purchased for him. Her daughter, Betty, who
outlived Cora's other children, became his lifelong friend. He looked
upon Betty more as a sister than a cousin, and his relatives accepted
Paul's addition to their family as a most natural family event.

For those outside the family, however, an aura of mystery hovers over the reason a widowed father would give up an older child in favor of an infant who would surely require more care. Without doubt, Paul Barrus was loved and cared for as a child, but his relationship with his father seems to have been a strained one. Shortly after Daisy's death, his father re-married and continued to live with his new wife in the same town. Although Paul Barrus often spoke and wrote of his youth and the people he knew well as a child, he had very little to say about his father. In later years, Father Henry Petter tried many times to get him to talk about his father, but Barrus could never bring himself to reveal more than these barest facts: "My father, brother, and I lived in the same town, and we saw each other every week while I was a child, but it wasn't the same anymore. He soon remarried and eventually had eight more children." Apparently Paul Barrus never spoke of these half-siblings to his friends in later years, nor did he leave any written account of them that could be found. Whatever reasons there may have been to cause such a gulf between this man and his son remain unclear even to this day.

In a talk with Father Henry, Barrus recalled his father as "prim and proper, a tea-time sort who always wore a necktie, and was a bit stuffy." Without revealing particulars of the event, Barrus told Father Henry he had attended his father's funeral in 1952. He also had this to say about his father, "When I was four years old, my father bought a little blackboard and announced that it was time for me to learn the alphabet and, eventually, how to read." His father also taught him how to count and to do simple arithmetic even before he started school at five. "He took me later to the public library and told me to select a book," Barrus continued, "I chose *Little Black Sambo*, reading it again and again. It wouldn't be allowed nowadays because of what would be considered its racial overtones, but I loved it, and I never thought that he was a different color from me."

This mention of *Little Black Sambo* reminds me that it was also the first book I ever read. I enjoyed it in 1937 fully as much as he had in 1907. Are today's children deprived of the opportunity to know this wonderful book? I decided that a trip to the local library was necessary in order to learn the fate of *Little Black Sambo*. I learned that there was a period of about thirty years when the book was considered to be racially insensitive and a time during the '60s and '70s when several libraries, under considerable pressure, actually removed it from their shelves. It is of great help if one knows that this story of a dark-skinned child's adventures with four tigers was written in 1898 by Helen Bannerman, a white Englishwoman living in India during the ascendancy of the British Raj when the natives were commonly referred to as "niggers." That probably explains why the American version of the book was titled *Little Black Sambo*. The good news is that Sambo is back, not only in the version I remember, but there are also two recent, newly-illustrated editions that ask readers to reassess the story: *The Story of Little Babaji* (Harper Collins, 1996) and *Sam and the Tigers* (Dial, 1996). Although Bannerman sold her rights to the original publisher for a pittance, the book has never been out-of-print.

Barrus said this of his brother in a talk with Father Henry in the late nineties: "My brother Dale was very different from me. He worked at a bank in Winterset when he grew up, and when the bank was robbed, he chased down and caught the thief. Dale was a hunter. When he went to war, his wife proved untrue. He married again and had one son. I last saw Dale in the late seventies. He now lives in California in a home for the blind. He just turned ninety."

Surely the traumatic, early death of Paul Barrus' mother had an influence on his own great fear of dying, even at the age of ninety-seven. And the early estrangement from his father may have precipitated his life-long fear of being abandoned, which became particularly irrational in his advanced years.

By all accounts, the major influences which shaped the development and character of the young boy came from the maternal side of his family, i.e., the families of Mary Wells and Asbury Clopton, Daisy's parents. A brief look at their histories might shed light not only upon the era in which he was raised, but also upon the factors which contributed to the man he became.

A short history of the hard-working pioneer family of Daisy Barrus begins with her paternal grandfather, Robert Clopton, who came from England to Virginia. As a young man, he was an idealist. When the friction between the sections of the country began, contrary to his environment and to some of his family's opinions, he became an abolitionist — unpopular in a Southern state.

Like many Southern people who shared his views at this time,

Robert Clopton traveled westward. His first stop was in Kentucky, where he married Priscilla Davis. Together they moved to Missouri, then, with a young family in tow, went on to the free state of Iowa, where, as Paul Barrus tells us, "In 1862, forty years old and the father of five children, he enlisted in the Union Army. When I was a little boy, I heard my own grandfather talk about taking his baby brother in his arms and walking up to where the soldiers were assembling in the courthouse yard, and my grandfather watched his father, Robert Clopton, march away to the South. He never came back."

This sudden departure of his father left eleven-year-old Asbury Clopton (who would, in turn, become the father of Daisy Barrus) as the main support of his widowed mother, brothers, and sisters. According to a short, handwritten note found in the Barrus papers, the hardships this particular family endured were staggering: "Priscilla took in washing, and it frequently happened in cold weather that she returned to her brood of little ones after nightfall with her wet clothes frozen stiff."

One particularly interesting anecdote included in that note concerns an enterprising Clopton son who trained the family's calves to pull the wagon because they had no horses. This son was also able to make some money by using his calves and wagon to haul limestone to be used in the construction of Winterset buildings.

Barrus has said he was proud of his father's English heritage:

> I have visited England three times because it was
> the home of my ancestors. On one visit, I went to a
> 15th century church where lies the body of Sir Hugh
> Clopton, a distant relative. I had my picture taken
> by his tomb. I went to the cemetery there and found
> the graves of innumerable Cloptons, originally De
> Clopton, who came from France with William the
> Conqueror in the 11th century.[12]

Although he was proud of his English heritage, it was his Irish grandmother, Mary Wells, having married Asbury Clopton in Madison County, Iowa, in 1875, who made the most lasting impression on him. Her grandparents had migrated from Ireland, and it was her grandfather, Daniel Wells, who had hauled limestone from nearby quarries to build the Madison County courthouse.

When one considers that Barrus eventually became a Ralph Waldo Emerson scholar and an outstanding teacher of Emerson's work for many years, it seems prophetic that this maternal grandmother, Mary Wells Clopton, bears so much resemblance to Ralph Waldo Emerson's great aunt, Mary Moody Emerson, who figured hugely in Emerson's young and motherless life, as did Mary Wells Clopton in the life of Paul Wells Barrus. Just as Emerson dedicated much of his writing to his great aunt, Barrus dedicated his small book, *Moments of Grace*, to his grandmother: "To Mary Wells Clopton who showed me the way."

On each Decoration Day, originally a Civil War remembrance which we now know as Memorial Day, the young Paul Barrus accompanied his grandmother on an early morning walk to the Rock City Cemetery to decorate the graves of family members with fresh flowers the Clopton neighbors allowed him to clip. Barrus recalls:

> On those May mornings before 1917, Grandma and I were up early to avoid the heat of the day, for it was a long walk from our house to Rock City Cemetery. Once we were there in time to hear old Major Baxter giving a speech about the brave boys in blue that had "put down the rebellion an' saved Old Glory from being rent in twain."[6]

These visits gave Grandmother Mary many opportunities to teach the young Paul about the lives of their deceased kin as she walked from grave to grave telling stories about each one. Sometimes she would address the deceased one directly, as Barrus recalls in this story:

> "Here you are, Charlie," she said as we stopped near a weather-stained stone that was sunk far under ground. One could barely read the name — Charlie Wells, her brother who had died of consumption in 1871 at the age of nineteen. "You started to walk across the kitchen floor," she spoke toward the grave. "Mother was sick in bed, but she could see with her bedroom door open. She yelled, 'Catch him Mary,' as you commenced to fall. An' I caught you. You just gave a little gasp and were gone."

It was during those cemetery visits that Barrus' grandmother tried to teach him not to be afraid of death. "What is there to be afraid of? Remember child, it's the living that will hurt you, not the dead," Mary Clopton told him. This appears to be one of the few "Grandmother lessons" he did not take to heart.

A characteristic of people reared in Madison County, even though they may have died in distant places, is that they are always brought back to be buried in the home cemetery. "My great-grandmother, great aunts and uncles, second cousins, whole families are buried in Winterset," Paul Barrus said, and he, himself, was no exception. Although he worked most of his life in his adopted and beloved state of Texas, and though he died there as a very old man, he, too, now rests beside his young mother in the family plot in Winterset.

He has described his grandfather Clopton as a very kind-hearted man, but, "He always had a very negative, pessimistic outlook on life, and that had a profound effect on me as I grew up. I was always serious-minded — took life seriously, and looked more on the dark and heavy side, not the light side," Barrus told Father Henry. About his grandfather, he shared this story with his colleague friend, Carroll Adams: "When I was a little boy, my grandfather told me, 'See that tree. When that last leaf is gone, so will I be!'" Commented Adams, "Imagine the impact of such a statement on a bright, sensitive child whose mother was well and happy one day, holding her son on her lap, and before the next morning sun rose, she was gone."

Another time, the boy, Paul, and his grandfather passed by an old lady who was gathering sticks for building a fire. When the child expressed compassion for her, and a desire to help, his grandfather responded, "Don't waste any sympathy for her, child. She was known to have been a Copperhead." (This was a Civil War term used in the North to describe a Confederate sympathizer.)

Perhaps his grandfather's dark moods and his mother's sudden death did have a profound effect on him as he grew up because, although it was not widely known, Paul Barrus suffered bouts of depression throughout his life, and these encounters with life's darkness probably had their origin in his childhood.

Author William Styron, who suffered from severe depression, which began its most visible manifestations in his sixtieth year, has written in his lucid memoir, *Darkness Visible, A Memoir of Madness*: "To most of those who have experienced it, the horror of depression is so overwhelming as to be quite beyond expression." He calls depression "a wimp of a word for such a major illness." Although the disease is still not completely understood, Styron believes it originates in a sense of loss. Of his own case, Styron says, "The morbid condition proceeded, I have come to believe, from my beginning years—from my father, who battled the gorgon for much of his lifetime.... The genetic roots of depression seem now to be beyond controversy. But I am persuaded that an even more significant factor was the death of my mother when I was thirteen." [8]

Although it is fairly certain that the genesis of depression is not in all cases the same, the similarities here are significant: both Barrus and Styron were highly intelligent and extremely sensitive men, both had male progenitors who suffered from depression, and both had young mothers who died suddenly and unexpectedly. Both were also blessed with finding supportive, understanding partners who helped them through the worst of times. For Styron, it was his wife. In the life of Paul Barrus, it was his closest friends (in particular, Father Henry Petter) who played this role.

610 N.E. 17th Street
Grand Prairie, Texas   75050
FROM THE DESK OF

PAUL W. BARRUS
Wednesday noon, May 20, 1987

Dear Betty,

Here is a child's voice
out of the past -- a
letter written to Aunt
Will, in Atlantic, Iowa,
the year I was finishing
the second grade in the
Winterset schools --- 78
years ago this spring.

Maybe you will want to
keep it among your
souvenirs. "Backward,
turn backward, O Time
in your flight; Make me
a child again just for
tonight. .... Mother,
come back from that
echoless shore."

    Love,

    Cuz

On the following pages is the letter that accompanied this note

-1-

Winterset Iowa May 25 th 1909

Dear aunt

We reiceived your letter several days

ago

How are you all getting along

We have been haveing showers here

We thought we were going have a wind—

storm

We have been haveing bad weather here

The gardens are doing fine

Grandmas beans are up

When are you coming over

When you come bring the kids

I want to see them so bad

Be sure and come this saturday night

We will be at the train to meet you

Is Anthony good in school

hope he is

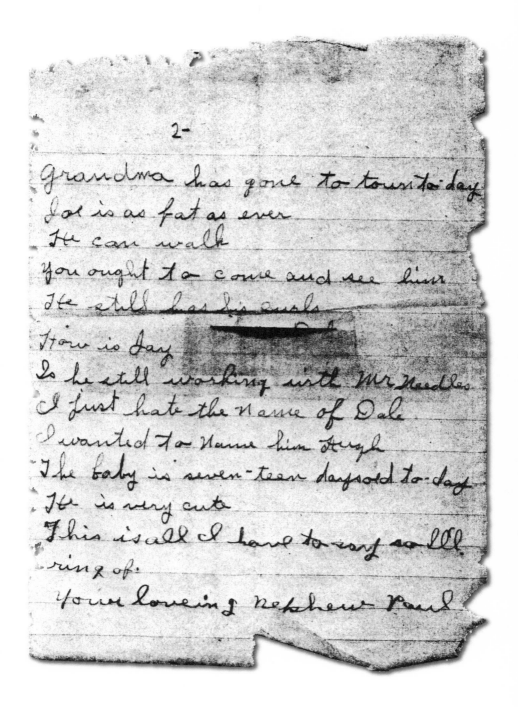

2-

grandma has gone to town to-day
Joe is as fat as ever
He can walk
You ought to come and see him
He still has his curls
How is Jay
Is he still working with Mr Needles
I just hate the name of Dale
I wanted to name him Hugh
The baby is seven-teen days old to-day
He is very cute
This is all I have to say so I'll
ring of.
        Your loveing Nephew Paul

More About the Winterset Paul Barrus Loved

The name of Winterset, Iowa, always fascinated Paul Barrus. It was there he was born June 29, 1902, and there he was buried January 11, 2000. A familiar name to many because of Maxwell Anderson's play by that title, Winterset as depicted by Anderson had no relation to the hometown Barrus recalled as the county seat of Madison County, Iowa, located thirty-five miles southwest of Des Moines. Nor does Robert J. Waller's 1992 popular novel, *The Bridges of Madison County*, contain characters bearing much resemblance to the Winterset people he remembered, according to a review of the book Barrus wrote in 1993 for *The Commerce Journal*. (That book review gives great insight into Barrus' philosophy of life, and it will be examined more closely in a later section of this book which discusses his own writing.)

In the following passages Barrus records fond memories of the Winterset town square of his childhood:

> Fifteen-cent ice cream sodas at the Candy Kitchen on the east side of the square (a favorite hangout for teenagers), pie suppers and box suppers in the country schools to raise money for books and other supplies, the annual visit of "Uncle Tom's Cabin" show with Little Eva driving her ponies in a parade around the square, and the venerable Mr. Cooper, a Civil War veteran who appeared in the high school on Lincoln's birthday to give an eyewitness account of Pickett's charge at Gettysburg.[6]

Court trials in Winterset often provided entertainment for those who had time to attend them. Barrus remembered hurrying to the old courthouse after school to witness a murder trial and listening "to the impassioned oratory, for and against the defendant. Once a lawyer pointed his hand dramatically toward the accused and cried, 'There sits the murderer of...'."

In his recollections of Winterset things past, he remembered when the Morrison family moved there, and when he saw little Marion Morrison (better known to us as John Wayne) being wheeled in a baby carriage by a neighbor girl along South Second Street; Barrus was then five years old. He also remembered John Wayne's father had worked in the drugstore on the west side of the square, and that his mother, Mrs. Morrison, was a "peculiar woman who had very few friends in Winterset." She was, Barrus remembered, "quite distant, and it was rumored that she smoked cigarettes!" He also recalls

> … waiting for the train at 4:40 p.m. to see who came from and who went to Des Moines; seeing the diamond-back rattlesnakes on display in the window of Krabiel's Drug Store on the southwest corner of the square; swimming au naturel in Ten-foot, a "swimming hole" in Middle River; going to home funerals and "sitting up with the dead" one or two nights before the services; and trying to shake, at the age of six, the cannon ball off the Civil War memorial in Monumental Park, just east of the square.

Reminiscent of Mark Twain's description of Hannibal in his youth, Barrus writes: "On Saturdays in the early 1900s, Winterset came alive with activities on the town square. Farmers arrived early to do their trading, townspeople came in to pay their grocery bills, and everyone went to the movies on Saturday night."

Paul Barrus, like many other young boys of this era, had jobs when he was not in school. "When I was twelve years old, I candled eggs at Carey Brothers. This involved letting light shine through the egg to determine whether it was fresh…. I, too, delivered groceries and had first-hand knowledge of many Winterset kitchens."[12]

All was not work, though; young people made their own fun:

> In winter, when the snow was deep and hard-packed, those of us who lived in town had a field day. We "hopped bobs," — that is, we'd stand on the runners of sleds homeward bound, ride to the outskirts of town, and catch another "bob" back to the square. The farmers were tolerant and so were their families sitting comfortably covered in blankets as the driver cracked his whip and grinned at our efforts to hang on.

As a child, he played in the woods around Winterset with three friends, and each summer he attended the plays of traveling stock companies passing through Winterset. He remembered seeing

"Tempest and Sunshine" in particular because he had found the book by the same name and had read it without telling his grandmother. He recalled that it cost a dime to sit in the bleachers during a performance, and a quarter to sit in a chair. Once, during a performance of *Uncle Tom's Cabin*, during a crucial moment when the stage crew was about to lift Little Eva up to heaven (using behind-the-scenes wires), a lightning bolt knocked out the lights, and that night they didn't get to see Little Eva swept up to heaven, a real disappointment to the cousin who attended the performance with him. Years later, when Barrus told his college students this story, he was shocked to learn that they had never heard of *Uncle Tom's Cabin*.

He remembered a popular girl in his high school who became sick with a pain in her side. They sent for the doctor and found him playing checkers in one of the stores. The doctor said, "Oh. It's just a stomach ache" and he did not leave his checker game. Barrus recalled, "Her appendix burst, and she died. I remember that was the first death of someone my own age. It impressed upon me the briefness of life."

He also recalled that there were two blacksmith shops in town. "One was owned by a man named Reese, and the other one was owned by the Wilkinson brothers. It was my duty to take my grandfather's horses to the blacksmith shop. I loved to see the blacksmith take the horse's hoof in his hand and nail on the shoe."

The amount of detail he remembered after so many years seems unreal to a person of this century. Barrus gave a clue, however, about the perennial freshness of his memories, when he said, "In my mind's eye, I like to go around the square and visit the various shops and stores that are forever gone."[12]

However important the town of Winterset was in the early life of Paul Barrus, it was Winterset schools and its teachers which molded and shaped him to become a great teacher himself. Most people cannot remember, as clearly as he did, their early school days and such lucid descriptions of teachers, classes, and learning experiences from the time he was five years old. His extraordinary memory and the habit of writing things down make history come alive for today's readers.

From First Grade to High School Graduation

It is now 1907. For the most part, Barrus remembered his early school days in Winterset with great pleasure. In these excerpts from more than one of his interviewers, one can gain real insight into the early forces shaping his character:

> The day I was five years old and started school, I said to my mother, "When I grow up, I want to be a teacher." My first teacher's name was Miss Edith Tate, and she spoiled me. My legs were too short for my feet to reach the floor, so she gave me a box to put my feet on. The first day of class Miss Tate asked "Who can make the figure eight?" Well, I saw my chance to shine because my father, before I started school, had bought a blackboard and had taught me how to do simple reading and writing."[3]

Barrus once recalled that while he was visiting in Iowa and having dinner with his cousins in a restaurant many years after he had been a Miss Tate student, a white-haired lady approached him, and asked, "Are you Paul?" "I said, 'Yes,' and then I took another look at her and said, 'You're Miss Tate'." When asked what made Miss Tate so special, he said: "Her warmth, her overlooking a childish fault, always trying to see something good in her pupils." Not so coincidentally, "always trying to see something good" in his own pupils, from first grade to post graduate, was a characteristic most frequently mentioned by former Barrus students interviewed for this book.

Some of his other teachers, he remembered in less flattering terms, although not less clearly. Here, he has this to say about some of them:

> My second grade teacher gave a rude shock. She was tall with a triangular face and discouraged my attempts to establish the rapport I had known with Miss Tate. The only carefree time I remember in the second grade was when we played a game and sang, "Have You Seen the Muffin Man?"
>
> My third grade teacher once descended on me

because I became enamored of a blue-eyed siren named Vivian Knowles, who sat across the aisle from me. One day, I committed the unpardonable sin of whispering to the lovely Vivian. It was then that my teacher descended on me. "Were you whispering?" she demanded. "Nnno," I stammered. She gave me a piercing look and then passed reluctantly on. My conscience immediately began to reproach me.

"You've told a lie," I said to myself. The issue was clear. I had to confess. I raised my hand timidly and said, "Miss Perkins, I was whispering." She took off her glasses, rose from her desk, came back to my seat and slapped me soundly. Thus I learned early that the way of the transgressor is hard.

At another time, he said of this same teacher:

She was not a young woman, and I was in mortal terror of her. But she taught me. When we were learning to multiply, she used to draw a circle on the blackboard and put numbers up to 12 around it. Then she'd put a large number like 8 in the center of the circle. She had a pointer. We might have the "8s" and she would point to 9 on the circumference of the circle. If you didn't say "72" you might as well stop living because she froze you with a gaze.[3]

Although few can remember childhood incidents as clearly as Paul Barrus, most have lasting memories of some insult suffered early which continues to rear its head at the most inopportune time, such as this one concerning his fifth grade teacher:

Before the term was over, she had whipped everyone in the room. She had a little rubber hose about a foot long. She whipped me twice with the hose: once for dropping my pencil on the floor, and the second time for coming into the schoolhouse after smelling the yellow of dandelions and getting pollen on my nose. Years later, when I was eighteen and teaching

in a one-room country school, she was the county
superintendent, and she came to visit me and my
school. I was so paralyzed that I could not teach!

His eighth grade teacher in North Ward School was a woman whom
he remembered as a disciplinarian and a fanatic on grammar:

She wouldn't be allowed to teach now because she was
a prescriptive grammarian. She taught us such things,
when I was twelve years old, as the three moods of
verbs. Was it three? Let's see... indicative, subjunctive,
and imperative, and one she called potential. And we
had to conjugate verbs in all moods. She might say
to me, "Paul, conjugate the verb in the present tense
in the potential mood." Or, she might ask about the
subjunctive mood—the mood of improbability. And
in those days it usually started out in a conditional
clause. For instance, instead of saying, "If you are
the king of England, prove it," we'd have to put it
in the mood of doubt in the subjunctive and say, "If
you be the king of England."[3]

The highlight of eighth grade was the Friday afternoon spelling
matches: "I reveled in those.... I'll never forget one winter afternoon
when the tension was high because finally only two spellers remained.
I was on one side, and this very intelligent girl was on the other, but
she missed the word 'leviathan'—which I could spell. I'd never had
such a feeling of triumph in my life."

It was also in eighth grade when death struck close to home once
again. He had fallen in love (at a distance) with a fifth grader, Romaine,
with "long, russet hair." Romaine and her sister came down with
diphtheria that same year. A large, yellow sign, signifying that someone
who lived there had a contagious disease, was attached to their house.
Her sister recovered; Romaine did not. As Barrus remembers it:

I went to the railroad depot the night her body was to
be taken to a nearby town from which she had come.
While we waited in the cold and snowy evening, a
car drove up, and out stepped her mother, father,
and sister. They got on the train and went away,

25

and that was the last I saw of Romaine. I remember
trudging home in the cold, and wondering about
God's mercy.

Years later, I was driving past the town in which she
was buried and came to the cemetery. The thought
came to me, after all those years, that I should visit
Romaine's grave. And so I turned into the cemetery
gate. There was a large stone with the family name
on it, but I couldn't go any farther. I couldn't look
at the grave of my childhood sweetheart.[12]

At this time he must have remembered his grandmother telling
him so many years before as they stood beside their family plot in
the cemetery, "Don't be afraid of death, child." Most likely because
of his young mother's tragic death, he would always have a difficult
time facing its inevitability.

Because of his early introduction to the public library of Winterset,
the young Paul spent every spare moment in the library "despite the
many signs that said 'Silence' and the watchful eyes of Miss Adeline
and Miss Rebecca." He tells of one afternoon after school when, to
his delight, he discovered a new book of cartoons "which to my early
adolescent mind were irresistible." He tells of devouring the cartoons
with silent laughter when, suddenly, Miss Adeline hovered over him,
accusing him of laughing at her, of making fun of her, and threatening
to have him barred from the library. He felt ashamed, but nothing,
not even humiliation, could keep him from going back to that magic
place. After that incident, "Miss Adeline was all smiles, but they were
meaningless to me. Words have immortality and I remember hers
even now with a twinge of pain."

And to this little remembrance, Barrus attaches a heartfelt admo-
nition, "Let us pray for a moment of grace to speak kindly or not at
all. Let us this very day read the third chapter of the letter of James
in the New Testament."

As I sit at my desk today, I find that Dr. Barrus, in absentia, has
made me curious once again, and I rise to check the Epistle of James.
There, I read: "Wherefore, my beloved brethren, let every man be swift
to hear, slow to speak, slow to wrath: for the wrath of man worketh
not the righteousness of God."

On January 3, 1993, *The Commerce Journal* ran a feature story by Paul Barrus, "The Winterset High School I Knew," in which he looks back on a September day in 1919, his first day at South Ward School, which then housed the high school and the eight elementary grades for children from the south half of the town. He had completed the first eight grades at North Ward School.

Like most teenagers about to make this same transition, then and now, he was concerned all summer about entering high school in the fall:

> And now the day had arrived. I was there and almost tongue-tied with awe. On the desk before me lay a printed sheet offering three courses of study, namely, commercial, Latin, and English. The Latin course, as its title implies, was primarily designed for the college bound — an extremely small group in those days. In the freshman and sophomore years, the following courses were required, not "elected": English composition, rhetoric, ancient history, medieval and modern European history, algebra and plane geometry. The English curriculum resembled the Latin with the exception of the language requirement. English course students were required to take two years of a modern language, in this case, German.

To these three basic outlines of instruction, another had been added — the Normal Training Course, designed to give a modicum of training to those who aspired to teaching in the one-room rural schools (at this time there were more than one hundred such schools in Madison County). Normal training students, like their commercial classmates, took no foreign language, but home economics or manual training, botany, and agriculture, physiology and physical geography were required of the would-be teachers.

In the junior and senior years, the Latin students continued with Cicero and Virgil; the commercial classes became more or less proficient in bookkeeping, typing, shorthand, commercial geography, and commercial law; the normal training pupils concentrated on advanced grammar, so-called higher arithmetic, methods and, in their senior year, what was known as pedagogy or school management.

That Barrus chose at such a young age (he was thirteen) to take both the Latin course of study and the Normal training reveals an early glance at the prescience he was to show throughout his life. After all, he had come home from first grade the first day and said to his mother, "I want to be a schoolteacher." He often said that he always wanted to teach — that he had a passion to teach, and so it was that he began early to prepare for his life's vocation.

He recalls that his Latin teacher was the best in high school:

> She was a German woman named Mildred Roush.
> She had yellow hair and cold blue eyes, and she started
> out every class period in our Freshman Latin class
> by having us give the principal parts of a Latin verb,
> preferably irregular. She had an uncanny memory. If
> you gave the same verb two days in succession, she'd
> remember and tell you. I loved my Latin teacher. She
> gave me insight into the magic of words, especially
> those of Latin derivation. She was a teacher of the
> old school. I believe she was convinced of the value
> of her discipline.[10]

Here, Barrus could just as well be talking about himself. He loved language and worked diligently throughout high school to add words to his vocabulary. In his fourth year of high school, he became fascinated with Emerson and other early American writers. He was to pass on this same enthusiasm to generations of his college students.

Of his high school days, Barrus summed up: "All at once, it seemed, the calendar said May 1919, and people began referring to us as the graduating class." The class prophecy was read, and "The prediction was that I would spend time in Fort Madison and that I would accumulate seven wives." (Fort Madison was then, as it is now, a prison. Barrus was a model student. The reference to seven wives seems equally improbable considering the life-long celibacy of Barrus. One can read between the lines and almost hear his fellow students chuckling at their own cleverness.) In his reminiscences about his high school days, he mentions that some of the other students had teased him about his use of "big words." He had not yet turned seventeen when the class prophecy was read so he was probably smaller than most of the male students, but he left no mention that he might also have been teased because he was not athletic or robust and his arms and legs were somewhat gangly.

How he made the transition from high school senior to teacher in the span of one short summer is more understandable when one looks at the "normal training" as well as the Latin curriculum he pursued in high school. He also had to take examinations in about sixteen subjects to qualify for his teaching certificate.[3]

⁓

PART II

TEACHER, TRAVELER, STUDENT, SOLDIER

Early Teaching Days

ALTHOUGH HE HAD EARNED a teacher's certificate by the time he graduated from high school, the minimum age for teachers in Iowa was eighteen. Fortunately for him there was a shortage of country school teachers that year and he was allowed to begin teaching at the age of seventeen. Of that first teaching experience, he has said:

> That fall I began teaching a one-room country school called Pleasant Grove nine miles south of my home town, and I never enjoyed teaching more. I had only six pupils... Oh, it was wonderful. And one of the girls could play the old organ, and how we used to sing. The schoolhouse was in a little building situated on the top of a high hill, and in the wintertime—Oh, that was a hard winter—there was a coal strike, and I used to have to get to school early to gather up kindling and have a good fire in the big old stove. I walked a half mile from where I boarded. And the snow that winter was hip deep. The youngest little girl and the youngest little boy, who were in the first grade, would come on their ponies, and they'd be almost frozen. The little girl, Iris Boyer, used to be

so cold she was crying, and I used to hold her on my
knees around the fire until she thawed out.[3]

In this touching little story of how Iris thawed out, one can see how
the relationship of teacher to student has changed over the years. Many
contemporary teachers are wary of the legal ramifications of touching
a student, even through such an act of comfort and kindness.

Father Paul continues the story of his first students: "I had two pupils
in first grade, one in second, two in fifth, and one in seventh." Then
he named each one, citing a little about each child. He felt having
four separate grades in one room was not a bad thing, telling Father
Henry: "You would be surprised at how much the younger children
learned by listening to the older ones recite." (Based on my own learning experience in a one-room school, the opportunity to tune into the
more advanced classes was a great joy I remember quite well.)

These two brief stories of his first teaching assignment seem all
the more poignant when one reads what Barrus said of his practice
teaching experience in "the normal teacher training" in his essay on
"The Winterset High School I knew":

> It is interesting to note that we embryo teachers were
> given a minimum of actual practice-teaching. We were
> encouraged to observe the regular grade teachers at
> work, but it always seemed to me that the reception
> they gave us when we appeared in their classrooms
> was distant if not downright chilly.[10]

Incredibly, when he was ninety years old, he could recall a special
Saturday seventy-three years before when he had set out for his first
journey alone after he had earned his first monthly teaching salary
of one hundred dollars:

> It was a day in late October, 1920, the kind of day
> that comes only in Iowa; incredibly blue skies, a
> warm caressing breeze, scarlet and golden trees, and
> a dreaminess in the air that banished all thoughts of
> snowdrifts and below-zero temperatures that might
> lie ahead.
>
> I was not old enough to vote, but I held a teacher's
> certificate that enabled me to teach the seventh and

eighth grades in a small coal-mining town in the
southeastern part of the state. This was my first
venture away from home and the feeling of being
grownup was exhilarating. In the morning of that
day, I boarded the Chicago, Burlington, & Quincy
train for the eight-mile ride to Tracy, Iowa, where I
changed to another train for the fifteen-mile trip to
Oskaloosa, the county seat of Mahaska County.[12]

(If he had been seventeen at this time, the year would have been
1919 rather than 1920 as he remembered it.)

Compared to the Winterset he had left, this town was a metropolis.
Continuing with the story, he declares in childlike wonder and joy:

First I sat in the yard of the venerable courthouse and
with great interest studied the passers-by. At noon I
went to a café called the Canary Cottage for a deli-
cious meal consumed with delightful isolation. *I was
eating by myself in a strange city!* Later afternoon was
spent roaming through the department stores, making
the few purchases that my salary would permit.

His second teaching assignment was a five year stint in Hamilton,
Iowa, then a small mining town in the southeastern part of the state.
An incident that happened while he was there shows the mettle and
level-headedness he exhibited when barely out of his teens. Some of
the children came to him and said, "Did you know that tonight Buddy
Francis is going to hide behind the Odd Fellows building, and when
Rodney Phillips comes out, he's going to stab him?" (Buddy, their fellow
student, had been angered when the man, Rodney Phillips, "bearded"
him, which means that he had rubbed his beard against the face of
the boy in public and had caused others to laugh at him.) Barrus kept
the boy after school and told him what he had heard. "I said, 'Give me
your knife.' He replied, 'I won't do it.' Then I said, 'We'll sit here until
you do.' We sat while the long shadows of the short winter day fell in
the schoolroom. Finally, he put his hand in his pocket and drew out a
six-inch knife with which he was going to kill Rodney Phillips."[12]

Neither his own youth nor his inexperience stopped Paul Barrus
from holding his ground with that student. This brings to mind a

letter from a former student of his earliest teaching days who wrote to him, "You were about eighteen, and too slight of build to keep order, but you won us over by your determination that we were going to learn in spite of all else."

Soon after the knife incident, he was faced with a tragedy he could do nothing about. One of his seventh-grade pupils died of what in those days was called "black diphtheria." The house was quarantined and "We stood in the yard as the funeral services were held. I looked through the window at my pupil's coffin. He was a gentle boy and I loved him," Barrus recalled.

The death of this child, and the death of Paul Barrus' mother, both so sudden and shocking, made such an impact on him that he would never forget the specter of death. Understanding this helps us to see why such a devout man as Paul Barrus had such a difficult time facing his own death.

He never tired of telling stories of his early teaching days, and he stayed in touch down through the years, even to the year of his death, with many of his students and fellow teachers. Fred Tarpley says of his friend, Paul Barrus, "He kept up with more people than anyone I've ever known. He told me he simply could not let go of friends. A woman from one of his first classes attended many of the celebrations which honored him while he was at ET, and even after he had left." One of his very early junior high students flew down on May 13, 1972, to hear him give the commencement address, "The Furnished Mind." (This address is so unusual that I have included it in the Appendix to this book.)

Marie Frye Gage of Des Moines, Iowa, a friend and former fellow teacher from an early assignment, wrote to Barrus in 1998:

> Do you remember the time that we had a big snow-storm during the night? The next morning you walked ahead of me on our way to the schoolhouse, leaving your footprints in twelve inches of snow, and I followed behind you, leaping and jumping, trying to match your stride. If I had a fraction of the dedication and persistence and sense of responsibility you always exhibited; indeed, had I literally followed in your footsteps, I could have done more with my life.

Age 18, 1920

Paul in his "salad days," the 1940s

Paul and his cousin, Betty Van Hosen Gibson, Kappa Delta Pi Banquet, Spring 1936

This is a sentiment to which many of his former students, from primary to graduate, and most certainly, I, would respond, "Me, too!"

While teaching full time during those early years in country schools, he visited his grandparents in Winterset whenever possible and contributed to their support.

> During the time I was seeing after my grandparents, my grandfather became senile and wandered away from the house occasionally. I remember one day in particular. Finally I found him sitting on a street corner talking to two little girls. I told him that if he did that once more, I would move away, and he would never see me again. I hated to tell him that, but I had to get him to stop running off. He never did it again.[12]

After his grandfather's death, he rented an apartment in Des Moines and lived there with his grandmother in the summertime before he went back to teach in the fall. Letters from his grandmother to Barrus reveal that she was always concerned about his health and well-being. In January of 1931, he received a message saying his grandmother was seriously ill. On hearing this news, he reports:

> And so I dropped everything and went. I arrived there late at night. The snow was deep on the ground. It was bitterly cold. I went down to see the doctor to ask if there was any hope, and he was a most unsympathetic soul. So, I came away in despair. I sat by her side, sat on her bed, while she was dying. The last word she said was my name.[12]

Although he was a grown man by the time of his grandmother's death, he must have relived that night when he lost his own mother. It was Grandmother Mary with whom he not only had visited graveyards but had sold Fuller Brushes from door-to-door in order to make enough money to buy a rocker for the front porch of their house. This rocker now sits on her front porch, according to his cousin Hugh's daughter, Vicki Strief.

During the depression, his teaching salary was cut from $130 per month to $70 with no pay during the summer. He says he had "two pairs of good stout shoes and two suits. I lived with a saintly old German lady who cut down the amount of my board and room in keeping with the salary cut." Even with this meager salary, he was able to save enough to attend summer school at Drake University for several years.

Winter/Teacher; Summer/Student

He received the Bachelor of Arts degree from Drake in 1933, having majored in English and Latin and having won many prizes: general scholastic honors, departmental honors in English, Phi Beta Kappa, Kappa Delta Pi (education), Eta Sigma Phi (classical languages), and Phi Sigma Iota (Romance languages).

Of his days at Drake, he said:

> I was fortunate enough to have the head of the department at Drake, an older man named Lewis Worthington Smith, for my freshman and sophomore composition. He was a Victorian gentleman of the old school and probably the best teacher of composition that I have ever seen or heard of. He had an absolute intolerance of sloppy thinking and sloppy writing. It was widely reported on the campus that if you used "like" as a conjunction in his class, you might as well drop the class. And I have seen him when the unsuspecting would say, "Well, it looks like it is going to rain today." And he would begin to tap on the table with that faraway look in his eye.[3]

What would be the response of Lewis Worthington Smith, or Paul Barrus, to today's "Valley Girl Speak" such as "Like me and my girlfriend like went to the mall, and then my mother was, like, really mad… and I was like…

His wisdom in choosing a double course of study in high school had paid off. Barrus was thirty-one years old and had already taught for fourteen years by the time he received his first college degree. He was earning $93.50 a month teaching English and Latin in high school when Drake University called and asked him to take advantage of the National Youth Recovery Act by teaching Latin there while working on his master's degree. Thus it was that he moved back to Des Moines in 1935. He stayed with relatives there who were also struggling financially. They all pitched in, and somehow like so many others at this time, they were able to survive. He taught nine hours of Latin that year at Drake, took a full load of graduate courses in Latin and philosophy, and wrote his thesis on "The Timeliness of Horace's Philosophy." Then, in the spring he was awarded a Lydia Roberts Fellowship for three years of study in Latin at Columbia University. "But," he said, "I had worked too hard. I had to rest for awhile so I turned down the fellowship."[10]

That summer of 1935, he took a one-month camping trip with a small group of friends and fellow teachers. A 160-handwritten-page spiral-notebook account of that trip, found in his private papers after his death, not only explains his attitude toward New York City as it was at this time and the probable reason for his rejection of the Columbia scholarship, but it also gives us a rare glimpse of Paul Wells Barrus behaving in maturity before the mantle of Catholicism, professorship, doctoral study, and other influences fell on his shoulders. It also gives a clear picture, not only of his state of mind at this point in time, but a luminous portrait in lucid prose of this particular part of the United States of America as seen through his eyes at this particular time in history. Far too lengthy to include here in its entirety selected excerpts from this diary should suffice.

Excerpts from 1935 Travel Journal

On August 3, 1935, Paul Barrus and a man he identified only as Tony set out in a 1929 two-door coupe from Boone, Iowa, destination not revealed. (In a childhood letter which Paul Barrus wrote to his "Aunt Will," he refers to her son, evidently about his own age, as "Anthony." Presumably this "Anthony" is the same person as the "Tony" of this travel journal.)

In Hamilton, Iowa, they were joined by another man, Clarence Martin, who drove a truck rigged with cooking equipment. Soon a fourth man, Walter, who was accompanied by three or four women, usually identified in the journal entries only as "the girlies," joined the procession. Barrus picks up the story here:

After we crossed the Mississippi at Burlington,
the boys "stepped on it" and the beautiful Illinois
woodlands, cornfields, and pastures fairly flew by. I
was impressed by the spick and span appearance of
the Illinois homesteads. Most of the houses, many
of Civil War vintage, are freshly painted and the
velvety green lawns and hedges are kept carefully
clipped. It was dark when we reached Springfield,
Illinois, a city rich in memories of Lincoln.

On the outskirts of Springfield, they set up camp for the night.
Unfortunately, they were camped close to some midnight revelers
"who made whoopee until the break of day." He comments, "Liquor
flows like water in Illinois, less subdued than in our own state of Iowa.
I wonder how much repeal has accomplished."

His impressions of the South, revealed in this next quotation, are
surprising in light of the fact that he was destined to live so many
good years of his long, successful life in the South — in the Southwest,
to be precise: "The landscape is much different from that of our own
Iowa prairies. Hills and timber, squat little houses, mostly unkempt,
perched on stones. Arriving in Nashville, I suffered no regrets that
I hadn't remained in school there. Grandma used to say, 'They are
do-less to the nth degree.'"

Outside of Nashville, the group set up camp for the night but soon
learned that the place was "infested with a gang of 'shanty Irish' who
evidently made their homes in tents there. Squalling babies, blaring
radios, cursing men, and barking dogs created a nightmare."

Throughout the trip, the Barrus group prepared all of its own
meals; each one was dutifully recorded in his journal. Clarence was
the cook; Paul, the dishwasher. When on the road at noon, they
always "munched" on sandwiches and drank "cool-aid" (which he
spelled with a "c" throughout the journal rather than a "K" as it is
currently spelled.) As the official drink at every meal except breakfast
when they had coffee, "cool-aid" was a variable in so many different
flavors that Tony complained at one point his urine had taken on the
colors of the rainbow.

Tony was the auto repairman; Walter's main function at first seemed
to be as chauffeur to "the girlies," but as the trip continued, Walter

began to get on the nerves of Paul and Tony who began to refer to him as "The Lord." Nothing much in the line of teamwork seemed to be expected from "the girlies." They had their own separate tent, and the men bunked together; Tony and Paul shared one tent, Walter and Clarence in the other.

The drive from Nashville to Chattanooga was pleasant until they reached the foothills of the Cumberland Mountains, where Barrus thought about the "boys in blue and the boys in gray" as they traversed this land once soaked in the blood of those "boys." The slower manner of these "Southerners" seemed to irritate Barrus greatly: "Tony says he's going to buy a rocking chair and move back to the South. *Not for me — ever.*" (*emphasis mine*)

In Knoxville, the group had a pleasant camping experience. The De Armand family who owned and managed the campground, invited them inside the family home to shower and do their laundry: "I shall always remember De Armand camp as the place where Marian Bronson, one of our party who teaches in Ames, went off in a little grove and 'vocalized.' She is a music teacher and is to give a recital upon her return to Iowa. A little Tennessee urchin across the road responded derisively to her efforts."

It was when they reached Virginia that he became almost ecstatic:

> What a beautiful state is Virginia! The poorest cottage
> is painted and its yard is bright with flowers. We are
> now driving northward through western Virginia. I
> have never seen a prettier countryside. The Blue Ridge
> Mountains and the fertile valleys make a picture I'll not
> soon forget. We couldn't help but notice the contrast
> between Virginia and Tennessee. As we drove along,
> we sang, waved and shouted at passersby.

In Washington, D.C., they found a good campground occupied by congenial folks, and they visited all the popular D.C. sights that people still visit and talk about today. In addition, he wrote: "We visited the Senate and listened to a few speeches. Senator Huey Long was sitting on the very front row on Vice-President John Nance Garner's left."

Paul Barrus recorded everything that came to his attention on this trip in such meticulous detail — even such minutiae as in this description of his laundry:

> After we returned to camp, I washed (on a scrub
> board) 2 white shirts, 2 polo shirts, 3 prs. socks, 2
> undershirts, 2 prs. shorts, and an extremely dirty
> pair of trousers. In the afternoon I rigged out an
> ironing board in the rear of the truck and ironed my
> clothes…. After the supper things were done we sat
> and discussed President Roosevelt, child opportuni-
> ties, school teachers and what not.

He had this to say of Baltimore: "As it did last year, Baltimore impressed me as an ugly city, crowded and congested…. My country soul
recoils from the artificial life of these huge hives." Of rural Maryland,
he had a much higher opinion: "One can tell that it is a long-settled
country. The fields and hedgerows, and even the pasture lands and
timber have a trim, well-kept appearance, silent evidence of the long
struggle of man to mold and subdue his natural environment."

In Pennsylvania, he conversed in German with an old Pennsylvania
Dutch gentleman until they were interrupted by two drunks one of
whom, Barrus said

> is planning to take a car and go on an all-night spree,
> since his wife has gone away — thus releasing him
> from the chief civilizing influence of his life. Such
> morons should be restrained and prosecuted for
> they are a menace to life. One youngish clean man
> standing nearby remarked that it was deplorable that
> they should drive while intoxicated, but dismissed
> the matter by stating that "Every man has to work
> out his own problems."

As they crossed into New Jersey, the travelers were becoming a
little edgy with each other: "We've been mocking a member of our
party who has the habit of saying, 'What is it?' to every query whether
she hears it or not. We really shouldn't, but her peculiar inflection is
side-splitting."

In New York City, he found some of the subway riders startling:
"Two girls talked like phonographs while chewing gum and batting
their eyes. A suspiciously blonde creature in a lavender dress with huge
spectacles, a pancake hat, and roving, bulging eyes scratched her leg
zealously just across from me."

41

While his friends took in a burlesque show, Barrus rode a double-decker bus to Riverside Drive:

> There I rested by the riverside to watch the lights come out on the Jersey shore. It was a beautiful sight. An excursion boat, ablaze with lights, floated on the dark waters like a huge firefly.... A father tossed a ball for his children while his wife screamed and scolded nearby; a burly tramp smoked a pipe and ate sandwiches like a gourmand in the shadow of some bushes, and always there was the rumble of the traffic on Riverside Drive above our heads. What a scene of human interest it was!

On Friday, August 17, 1935, he wrote from their Bronx camp site, "The whole city is mourning the death of Will Rogers and Wiley Post, who were killed in an aeroplane accident in Alaska on Thursday." On Sunday, they attended High Mass at St. Patrick's Cathedral. Of that Mass, he said, "The sermon concerned the benefits of the grace of God and what man deprived of that grace might be."

He found Coney Island to be thoroughly disgusting: "Coney Island is a living testimonial of an enervated, artificially stimulated, intellectually resource-less, self-doubting rabble." On the beach, he observed, "raw humanity seething, barrel-bellied women with ugly folds of skin hanging from breasts and hocks, scrawny, middle-aged men with sparse hair, wrinkled crones with pipe-stem legs" and so on. Amid all of this, he thought "of the pleasant prairies of the Middle West, the shady little towns, the shining corn rows, and the homely kindness of folks not too far removed from Mother Earth," and he admits he is weary.

On their return trip to Iowa, Barrus records that he sees some beautiful places, but it is with great relief that they cross the Mississippi into "the best state of them all!" The last entry is short. Dated August 30, 1935, it says simply, "Home at last! Words fail me."

This very personal travel journal answers to my satisfaction the mystery of why he turned down the prestigious award to study at Columbia University. Considering the deep affection he felt for his native Iowa and his abhorrence of large, impersonal places, it seems that New York City was simply too far from the Iowa womb, and thus, too threatening.

It also seems he was suffering some form of depression at this time. One of the generally acknowledged symptoms of depression, as discussed earlier, is complete exhaustion. It was in a state of exhaustion that he began this arduous month-long trip with his friends, and the travel journal certainly indicates he was more exhausted than exhilarated upon his return home. Although he had said he needed to rest for awhile, he did not "rest" for long after the road trip. That same fall he returned to public school teaching and continued graduate work in the summer.

University Teaching, Doctoral Studies, and Becoming Catholic

After having received his Master of Arts degree at Drake University in 1936, he was invited back there as an English instructor the following spring. From 1937 to 1941, he taught five classes of freshman English for $1,000 per year. He loved teaching at Drake because "The faculty dedicated their lives to teaching, and the classes were small. I still think that teaching without human relationships is barren."[10] (One wonders what he might say about the fairly recent concept of distance learning and on-line courses, were he alive today.) Those five years at Drake were happy years for him. He was now in a position to assist the Van Hosen family who had helped him when he first came there to study. He and his cousin, Betty Van Hosen Gibson, who worked for the dean at Drake and who also attended classes there, would have lunch and later walk home together after work. In his remembrances of those times, he talks about finding little restaurants which served good food for under a dollar. Through those lean years the closeness of this family seemed to bind them together. Paul Barrus loved being near his family.

Although I was unable to interview Betty (now deceased), she left a wonderful poem she wrote in 1987 about her cousin which reflects their closeness. Although Betty claimed to be no poet, she gave it her best effort. I have been told that her poem was read aloud at the Paul Wells Barrus Lecture Series Luncheon that year. Betty's daughter, Mary Jane, gave me permission to include it here:

A Jingle About Cuz for His Friends:
...To write about Cuz is really a pleasure.
I'll give it my best 'cause he's such a treasure.
As most of you know, he's more than a cousin.
He helped rear us all, well over a dozen.
He ever was faithful to grandparents, plus many
Who needed his help, which he gave of 'aplenty.'
He's completely contented in his second profession.
Now he stays busy hearing confession.
To me he has been a caring 'fourth brother.'
You see I had three, glad Cuz is the other.

Pat Van Hosen remembers times with Barrus in Des Moines: "I met Paul in 1938, at the same time I met his cousin, Hugh. The family was so close-knit that when I married Hugh, I married his whole family. In spite of the hard times, we had such fun. Someone would say, 'Let's go get a roach,' and that was our signal to pile into one or two cars and drive to the ice-cream parlor on Friday nights to get ice cream cones." (How the meaning of a word such as "roach" can change through the years!) Pat continues with her story, "Hugh worked in a bank, and he was instrumental in helping his family to initiate the loan which enabled them to buy a house." They jokingly called this bank, "The Van Hosen Survival Association," according to Pat. They called their house "The Iola Survival Society," says her daughter, Vicki Strief. They lived on Iola Street in Des Moines.

Pat says she will always remember that Paul Barrus, in spite of all his learning, never talked down to her even though she had not gone to college. In a 2006 interview, Pat said, "I am now eighty-nine years old, and we were in touch until his death. We never had any trouble communicating on any level. When we all got together as a group after having been our separate ways, it was always as if we had never been apart. He never changed. Paul had a unique place in the family."

The respect and affection with which Pat Van Hosen regarded him was most certainly reciprocal. A perusal of his last will and testament reveals that she was, along with Betty and her family, among his beneficiaries at the time of his death.

In 1941, he decided to take a year off and attend the University of Iowa to work on his doctorate. While there, in addition to the prescribed courses he would need to complete his advanced degree in English and American Literature, he also took courses in Latin and Greek, studied the ancient Latin hymns and read the *Confessions of St. Augustine*. It was in one of these classes that he met a fellow student, a Jesuit priest, who was also working for his doctorate in English. According to Barrus, "I became well-acquainted with him, and he instructed me in the faith. That year he baptized me and received me into the Catholic Church. I was forty-two years old, but I began to think about studying for the priesthood."[13]

To comprehend the trauma to a seven-year old who witnesses his much-loved mother's death is next to impossible for anyone who enjoyed a stable, secure family upbringing. It is equally difficult for non-Catholics to understand the role of Mary, the mother of Jesus. The concept of a divine mother was well established long before the onset of Christianity as a world faith. It was one of Catholicism's major contributions to the humanization of what had been, in its early years, a rather austere and millennial faith with the end time close at hand. One of the needs of the early church was a human face, and more important, a human heart, a mother of all humanity. Paul Barrus was not the first nor will he be the last to embrace a faith that comforts as well as commands, that reassures while it enforces a moral vision. He had lost an earthly mother but found her divine counterpart.

In 1943, any dream he might have had about becoming a priest came to a halt, as did his academic career, when he was drafted into the United States Army as a private. Although he was in his fourth decade—beyond normal draft age—he was single, in good health, had two degrees, and many years of teaching experience. One might assume the Army wanted him because of all his valuable experience as an educator. However, as one reads of his time spent in the Army, that doesn't seem to be the case.

The Army Calls; PFC Paul Barrus Answers

A more unlikely warrior than the gentle, peaceful Paul Barrus is hard to imagine. His students asked each other: "Do ya think he had to go to boot camp? Have his head shaved? March in formation? Do KP? Dig a foxhole? Shoot a gun? Watch those awful films about the dangers of VD?"

Private Paul Barrus did not begin his military life with any romantic notions about war. He had vivid recollections of Mr. Cooper, the Civil War veteran from Winterset, who came to his boyhood school every year on Lincoln's birthday to speak on the Battle of Gettysburg.... "He gave me in that speech an everlasting horror of war — a war that never should have happened," Barrus said.

He also remembered World War I and gave this first-hand report of that first Armistice Day celebration in Winterset:

> I was in high school, and I was on my way back to school after lunch. I had reached the Baptist church when suddenly all the whistles and bells in town began to blow. I went on to school and found ordinarily reserved teachers dancing up and down the aisles with the students. School, of course, was dismissed, and we all went to the town square where the Kaiser was hanged in effigy from one of the maple trees in the southwest corner of the square. Overshadowing this celebration, however, was the memory of those fellow students, just a few years older than I, who had gone to war in Europe and had never come back.[10]

One of the schoolmates he talks about here is a Bruce Croft. "I remember his father, Ross Croft, coming down the street in his wagon, crying aloud and screaming that his son was dead.... They told us in those days," Barrus continues, "that this had been the war to end all wars. Alas, here I am some twenty years later, involved in World War II."

Pat Van Hosen recalls, "When Cuz went into the Army, the commanding officer told him: 'I want to shake your hand. You scored higher on the tests than any one else ever has. Especially, you excelled in languages. Unfortunately, we have no need for those particular languages.' And so, he had to enter as a buck private."

Of a psychiatric exam all the recruits were required to pass before being sworn in, Barrus recalled, "The so-called examiner asked me, 'Do you like girls?' I said, 'I sure do.' Then he said, 'Go on.' That was my psychiatric examination." He also spoke of the time his sergeant told the men, "suck in your guts." Barrus followed orders and almost lost his pants. The commanding officer called him in and asked, "How come you let your pants fall down?" Barrus replied, "I've lost thirty pounds and they wouldn't stay up. That's how."[10]

First destination for new recruit Barrus was Camp Callan, adjacent to Camp Pendleton, a Marine base, south of San Diego. "The corporal in charge of the new recruits was a Chinese man who could barely speak English. Most of that was profanity." Barrus called another corporal at that base, "the greatest profanity artist of all time." No one he heard in later years, he said, could compare to this "artist."

It seems that he drew more than his share of KP duty. He told several of his friends in later years of the time he spent all of one Christmas Eve stuffing turkeys. At night, he fell exhausted on his cot. His buddies wouldn't let him sleep. "Get up! We have to go to midnight Mass!" they told him. "I can't get up. Just let me lie here and die," he answered. He did get up, and they all went to midnight Mass, thinking it might well be their last. According to Barrus, "I'll never forget that night. The Mass was said in Latin, and it left an indelible impression on me."

Something else left an indelible impression on him that Christmas Eve. As he explained it: "We went early to get a good seat, but before Mass began, the officers or 'brass' came in with their wives, and they asked us to move back to a less desirable position. I never got over that. To think that in the house of God, you had to give up your seat on account of the military caste system."[12]

Almost up to the time of his death, Paul Barrus could still recall clearly his first days in the Army. He remembered the names of the men, where they were from, and had all sorts of stories to tell about those first Army experiences. His cousins have said he got more than his fair share of teasing from fellow soldiers. He learned to take his rifle apart, but he had a terrible time putting it back together. He had a difficult time with many of the manual tasks that soldiers were expected to perform, and it's hard to imagine he might have taken part in any "female conquest" talk. A quiet-spoken, reserved, gentle man such as Paul Barrus could have been, and probably was, considered a "sissy" among men hell-bent on proving their manhood. He bore the brunt of many of his comrades' practical jokes with good grace, but at a certain point, his old bouts with depression returned, as can be seen in this letter he wrote to friends from Camp Callan, dated January 17, 1943. (The similarities between his state of mind expressed here, and those William Styron described almost fifty years later in *Darkness Visible* as the symptoms of his severe depression, are striking.) In the letter, Barrus speaks of an "apathy and dull pain that has robbed my expression," continuing in this same vein:

> It has been a strenuous and hopeless effort to compete physically with men fifteen and twenty years younger than I. The years have taken away my power of recuperation, and for some time I have felt myself slipping a bit each day. These nine weeks have been (May I say it without being sacrilegious?) my Gethsemane. How many times have I looked out over the cruel, relentless ocean or up at the star-sprinkled sky with a silent anguish in my heart that finally left me dazed and almost inert.

And yet, another note of despair from this same letter:

> Something has gone. I am too beaten to be bitter, too tired to be cynical, and too thoroughly crushed to be blasé. As I may have mentioned to you before, something with which I lived intimately almost ever since I had the gift of consciousness, is either dead or dormant. Maybe it's what Socrates called the "daemon." Life will never be the same again. The desire for solitude, to run away and hide myself like some hurt animal, would, if I didn't fight against it, become an obsession with me. I've always loved my fellow men, but now I'm afraid of them.

A close Barrus friend who is also familiar with the life and works of Flannery O'Connor speculates that it may have been then and there that Paul Barrus finally discovered his fundamental aloneness in the world: "It was probably related to his knowing that, like Flannery O'Connor, he was 'not homosexual so much as non-sexual,' and that this in turn meant that he would never know intimate love, whether in marital or familial life." In order to honor the very private Paul Barrus, I will not treat the matter any further.

This profound sense of aloneness became, one suspects, at least one of the sources of his religious doubts as well — doubts he sometimes suffered, and of which he spoke openly with his closest friends. (Are we finally alone in the universe? Are all of our convictions about God's nearness and dearness mere illusion that we have concocted to fend off the fact that "there is nothing but nothing" as Hulga Hopewell in O'Connor's "Good Country People," expresses it.?) People of great faith often undergo such trials. "When life got too hard in the Army, I went to the little chapel on the grounds of the base, meditated, and prayed to God. Oh, I said many prayers while I was in the Army," Barrus wrote.

Finally the Army "brass" decided he would make a good time-and-motion-study man. They sent him to work for Consolidated Aircraft Corp. in San Diego. This aircraft plant was completely covered with camouflage. "This was a job held in bad repute by the employees. They called us efficiency experts and worse names. I was sent out into the plant to study different operators and what they were doing and make a written report of their efficiency." He recalled one such study in particular. It was of a woman "of Amazonian proportions." When he walked up to her station, she said, "Listen, Bud, you ain't makin' no study of me." Thinking she might calm down and recognize that, like her, he was only trying to do his assigned job, he lingered awhile and tried to engage her in small talk. She laid her hand on a sledge hammer. "Listen, Bud, I mean it. You make a study of me and I'll let you have it."[10]

(As a student in his Development of the English Language class, I clearly remember his telling this same story. Like most of the anecdotes he told in his classes, this illustrated a point he wanted to make. This time it was about the levels of language. "Hers was the vulgate," he said, and this new word was etched with laughter in the minds of his students.)

After he was reassigned from time-motion study to reading blueprints, he encountered a different sort of problem. The women in this department were worried because he wasn't married. One of the women invited him to her apartment for steaks. "I don't eat meat," he told her, and then, in an aside, he added: "Well, part of that statement was true. I didn't eat meat on Friday. One day these same women grabbed me by the lapels and said, 'We want you to tell us why you ain't married.' In order to escape, I made up a tale about the tragic death of a fiancée so they would leave me alone."[10]

Asked once, many years later, if he had ever had any romantic flings, he answered,

> There weren't any flings. There was just one that I was greatly interested in. But my duties came first. That sounds rather priggish, but that's the way I looked at it. A part of the pattern.... I had helped to support my grandparents as they grew old. When my grandparents were gone, I was beyond the age when most people get married. I was embarked on an academic career.[3]

Finally the Army found the right spot for him: "They'd discovered I'd been to college. It takes the army some time to discover those things." From the aircraft plant, they sent him to Iowa State University to teach soldiers and sailors. "There I taught English. Not what you might call the finer points of English, but clear, direct communication," he said. He once told a class comprised of all sailors about the woman in the defense plant who "cussed like a sailor," and the whole group burst into laughter.

In late 1942, the U.S. Army found that it had too many over-age enlisted men who could not be sent overseas. Barrus knew, of course, that he was a strong candidate for an early discharge, but his personal letters during this period reveal that he was reluctant to leave military service when so many fellow soldiers could not. His correspondents urged him to get out as soon as he could, so on January 14, 1943 Private Paul Barrus was granted an honorable discharge.

Upon Leaving the Army and Completing Work on Ph.D.

Now a civilian, he returned to the University of Iowa to pick up where he had left off with his doctoral studies in English and American literature. In the summer of 1945, he took his comprehensive exams for the doctorate. Of this experience, he has said: "I wrote for a week. I still have my questions. I get them out once in awhile to see how many I can answer."

He did about three years of research on his dissertation, "Emerson and Quakerism," and finished it at midyear, 1948. One member of his doctoral committee called him back after his successful defense and asked him how it was that a good Catholic made such an unusual choice as Emerson for a dissertation study. His answer is enlightening. In it can be seen the essence and the openness of his thought processes, and it probably explains, at least partially, why he became such good friends with people of different faiths, or, in some instances, of no faith at all. "I always had the point of view that you should know something about other people's beliefs," he explained. This response was not simply a point of view for Barrus, it was more a way of life. A consensus of opinion among his friends reveals that he always listened with respect to others even though their views, whether religious, political, or social, might differ considerably from his own.

Emerson was a transcendentalist; Barrus was a Catholic who has been called a traditionalist. When asked if he felt "traditionalist" was a fair characterization of his philosophical belief, he responded:

> Well, traditionalist is a strange term. To many, tra-
> ditionalism is synonymous with stagnation, but to
> me, "tradition," coming from the Latin word "*trado*,"
> meaning to "hand down," has to do with those truths
> which the experience of humanity has proved to be
> valid and authentic, no matter what age. There's a
> universality about the Catholic tradition which I
> think is all-important."[3]

The two beliefs, transcendentalism and Catholicism, are, according to Barrus, "quite different doctrinally, but both are still basically God-centered. I am not a pantheist, as Emerson has been accused of being, but he was God-obsessed, and I think that is a good thing."

Dr. Ralph Wood, in an essay about Barrus for *The Christian Century*, says: "He wrote his doctoral thesis on Emerson, he once confided, in order to become a better Catholic. Only as he encountered the best secular literature—both affirming its insight and contesting its blindness—could his Christian faith remain vigorous and honest."

"When I went to take my Ph.D. examination in German for the doctorate, I didn't have any trouble," Barrus often told friends. The story of how he learned this language was one he liked to tell. In the late thirties, he was boarding with a German landlady while he was teaching English and Latin in a high school in Iowa. This woman had not known a word of English when she came to America. She had learned to speak English by sitting in the back of a church listening to the preacher while she held her baby in her arms. When she heard that her young boarder needed to learn German for his graduate studies, she offered to teach him. Every night she would get out the Lutheran Bible written in German. She would say, "Now we will read." If he mispronounced a word, he would have to try again. In the four years he was with this landlady, he learned to speak German fluently. From this time to the end of his life, he enjoyed engaging other German speakers in conversation at every opportunity. In particular, many of the friends he socialized with remembered that he loved speaking their language with the waiters and waitresses in German and French restaurants they frequented.

In 1948, with his newly won degree in hand, he decided to seek a position outside of Iowa, preferably in a state with a warmer climate, according to Fred Tarpley:

> The winters there were so severe, and he had so much trouble with upper respiratory infections and other difficulties caused by the cold, the doctors advised him to seek a warmer climate. I don't remember the details of the particular illness and hospitalization which led him to make the decision to leave Iowa, but at one point his condition was so severe, a priest was called in and he was given Extreme Unction.

He heard about an opening at East Texas State Teachers College in Commerce, Texas, and sent in his application for the open position. Dr. James G. Gee, then president of the small regional college, sent him a telegram saying he was appointed an associate professor for $3,500 per year. Barrus said of this offer, "In 1948, that was a fortune. I accepted the offer."

It is reported that General William T. Sherman was, for a time, stationed in Texas during the Mexican War. When asked his impression of Texas, he is said to have replied, "If I owned Texas and Hell, I'd rent out Texas and live in Hell!" As most Texans know, in August, Texas and Hell are indistinguishable. Perhaps unaware of Sherman's unflattering assessment, and at this time of year certainly not worried about heat in August, the newly minted Dr. Barrus set out by train from the blustery cold of Iowa winters, arriving at his new job and new home, in Commerce, Texas, on that bitterly cold day in January, 1949, recounted earlier and highlighted in a Texas folklore expression: "In winter, in Texas, there ain't nothing between you and the North Pole 'cept a bob-wahr fence in Dalhart!"

ⅽↃ

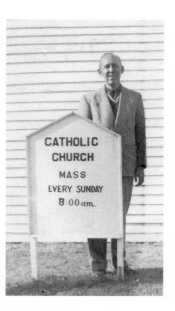

PART III

LIFE AS AN ADOPTED TEXAN

ET Commerce Story Resumed

IN SPITE OF THE COLD BEGINNING Paul Barrus experienced upon arrival at ET, warmth awaited not only in the change of seasons but in changes of attitude toward him and changes in the college itself.

Thanks to Dr. James G. Gee, a retired Army colonel, who had become the fifth president of the college on September 1, 1947, the dream that the school would rise above provincialism to become a first-rate university began with an effort to reach out to other places and other institutions of higher learning to attract the best teachers. When he was first hired, Dr. Gee told Barrus he was trying to get varied points of view to prevent the college from becoming too narrow in its outlook.

"He helped turn this college into a university," Barrus often said of Dr. Gee. During my interview with Dr. Carroll Adams, retired ET professor, Adams used the same words to explain the role Paul Barrus played in the evolution of ET from college to university. Both Barrus and Adams credit Dr. Gee with diversifying the faculty. "Before Gee, the faculty was mostly Southern, and many of the professors had other businesses or other interests, perhaps a farm or dairy, or some other occupation. Teaching wasn't always the principal interest. Dr. Gee changed that gradually from 1947 to 1966.

After World War II, beginning with the passage of the G.I. Bill, the student population at ET began to increase. A further increase came with the passage of a bill by the 1947 Texas Legislature which included new requirements for teacher certification. This meant that many already established teachers who did not meet those requirements would have to go back to college to make up any deficiencies in order to be re-certified. Texas public school teachers came to the campus by the hundreds after this legislation (known as the Gilmer-Aiken bill) became law. The less serious of these students became known around campus as the "Gilmer-Aiken bunch."[10]

Barrus was assigned to teach these students a course in modern British literature. He has said of this experience,

> The room was crowded to the walls, and the faces looking back at me revealed a variety of emotions. Some were eager; some were scared; a few were listless; two or three were defiant. One of the defiant, a lady, contained herself until we came to Evelyn Waugh. Then she went into action. Every time I asked for expressions concerning some point of view, her hand shot straight upward. Her comment was invariably *"Read your Bible!"* One morning, at wits end, I answered this admonition with, "Mrs. A., I *do* read my Bible. *In fact*, I'm reading and meditating on the book of Job at this very time. *His patience is a model for us all.*"[2]

(What irony! My bet is that it was lost on Mrs. A.) In a slightly different version of this same story, he reminded Mrs. A. that the Bible was not a textbook in modern British literature.

Coming to East Texas from Iowa to teach the Development of the English Language and its thousand-year literature must have been daunting for the scholarly Paul Barrus. His first classroom experiences at ET surely were the reality check that most teachers encounter at some time during their careers. For example, it is not all that unusual to find a certain number of ill-prepared students, and when that happens, the teacher has to fall back and regroup. If Paul Barrus fell back, he did not relax the rigor of his method. Like most effective teachers, he simply treated his East Texas farm boys and girls as cultivated adults. If, in fact, they were not, they quickly learned that they should aspire to what Dr. Barrus expected of them. In three years, Barrus had established quite a reputation on campus as being a top-notch professor with great expectations of his students. This notoriety did not escape Dr. Gee's notice.

Role of Barrus Grows Along With Growth of the College

In 1952, Dr. Gee called Barrus into his office and told him that he was to be head of the Department of English as of that day. Said Barrus,

> You didn't argue with Dr. Gee and his high ideals for the institution. He pounded on his desk and said, "Something has to be done about English on this campus, and I've hired you to do it." On his desk before him lay a letter from an alumnus containing many egregious errors. It began like this, "Both me and my wife is former ET students." "This has to stop," Gee continued. "I want you to establish a freshman English program that will make this sort of thing impossible."

Barrus continues,

> As a result of Dr. Gee's edict, I organized the following procedure. Every entering freshman wrote an essay that was evaluated by the English faculty. Two instructors read each paper. If the two readers disagreed, a third reader broke the tie. Those students whose essays were considered deficient were placed in a remedial English class which met five days a week for three semester hours' credit.

These requirements met with loud criticism from some students who openly protested the changes. For example, one young man stopped him on campus and threatened to bring him before the Board of Regents. "We persevered, however, with Dr. Gee's unwavering support," Barrus added. (Paul Barrus Day Address, April 24, 1995)

Several English professors from this era mentioned the difficulty of implementing this program of remediation, but praised the results. The story of the girl who reported, "That old English bunch was the reason I didn't get my teacher's certificate," was passed back and forth in amusement between members of the English faculty. Evidently "that old English bunch" had taken on additional tasks of extra essay grading and remedial work without complaint and were rewarded with better-prepared students.

Perhaps because of his varied experience teaching English (from first grade through high school, from undergraduate to graduate, from soldiers to factory workers) Barrus knew that standards *could* be raised. He knew how to teach the fundamentals as well as the more esoteric aspects of the mother tongue, and he treated the more and less advanced students with the same respect. He wanted students to do the very best they possibly could; at the same time, he recognized that not everyone is capable of abstract thinking,

> I'm very much in favor of vocational schools for people who can't profit by the so-called liberal arts courses, although I think everyone can profit from some aspects — English and History are two that I have in mind. If a man is a skilled auto mechanic, I have great respect for him, just as much as I do for anyone who is a master of his trade. We are all ignorant. We're just ignorant in different things.[10]

Just as interested in his more advanced students, Barrus worked hard to keep his Milton, Emerson, Thoreau, and Twain classes interesting and alive. Dr. Charles Linck says, "I came for my ET job interview in the summer while Barrus was teaching a Milton class. I was surprised; amazed to see thirty to forty students in a Milton class. I came from the University of Kansas, and I can tell you that any professor there would have been lucky to get three students in a Milton class in the summer time." Many Barrus students stayed with him year after year, taking class after class, and some of them followed him from the time they were students in his remedial classes all the way to graduation.

Another of the changes Barrus was able to bring about as department head was the re-location of the English faculty to one central location. The offices and classrooms of the English teachers were scattered all over the campus: in the agriculture building, in the old journalism quarters, in the science building, and in the home economics building. A beautiful new library, to be named for Dr. Gee, was under construction at this time. Barrus wrote to Dr. Gee and asked if the English Department could have the old library building so they could all be conveniently concentrated, and Dr. Gee agreed, telling him to go ahead with remodeling plans. The English faculty soon had their own special place at last. This charming old building was renamed the Hall of Languages, and students still meet there today for their English and foreign language classes. Barrus' papers are housed today in the archives of the Gee library. These enduring impressions reflect the lasting influences these two gentlemen had on ET through the years.

Dr. James Grimshaw, who came to the university years after Dr. Barrus retired, related this incident which also reflects, in its own way, the enduring influence of Barrus:

> I had met him, of course, because he came back often to visit his colleagues. I liked him instantly and felt a great rapport with him. When I became Head of the Department, I was assigned an office on an upper floor. I scurried around that day to find a comfortable chair and desk among a roomful of chairs and desks. A few days after I settled into my new office, Dr. Barrus paid me a surprise visit. When he walked in, he said, "You have my old chair!" And then, looking at the desk, he said, "There's a buzzer underneath with which you can summon the secretary." I reached under the desk, and as my fingers located the buzzer, the hair on the back of my neck rose.

Of such anecdotes as this did the legend of Paul Barrus at ET grow. In 1951, it was determined that the university needed a General Studies Program, and Dr. Gee notified Barrus that he had been designated as chairman of the committee which was "to begin work immediately and diligently to bring forth a 'general studies program' to be completed at the earliest possible moment." The group, working within a tight framework, met almost daily throughout the summer and then submitted their report to a steering committee.

The impetus for general education programs in Texas teachers' colleges had come from the Texas Education Agency which determined that students in teacher education programs were not receiving broad enough training in the liberal arts. For a more thorough discussion of this program, please see *Professor Mayo's College: A History of East Texas State University.*[7] Also, more in regard to the ET committee's role in creating the General Studies Program can be found in the joint interview with Drs. Paul Barrus, William Jack, and William Truax.[9] This interview centers on the role Dr. Clyde Arnspiger, retired executive vice president of Encyclopedia Britannica Films, played as Director of General Education interested in implementing a "social process" into this program.

Incorporating this "social process" into the newly created General Studies program presented problems for teachers—particularly for teachers of literature. Barrus explains the problem this way:

> Our courses were to be centered on what was known as the "social process," a series of "family values" around which all phases of human experience could be incorporated. As far as the social process is incorporated into literature, there is an old trite saying that might capture it best: "Literature is caught, not taught." When you begin to mechanize it, you kill it. When you deal with abstractions, you must take into consideration transcendental values.
>
> In 1957, there was a campus revolt against the "social process" as the "values" were called. Feelings ran high. Anti-general education flyers littered the campus and finally the Board of Regents met to arbitrate the dispute. When the air cleared, three department heads had quit their positions, and to me it seemed as if everyone was relieved to return quietly to our classes. The "social process" eventually faded away.[9]

Because of his close association with the General Studies program, Dr. Barrus was thrust into this debacle and yet maintained his decorum. Dr. Tarpley expressed it this way: "He didn't get openly involved in campus politics, yet everyone seemed to know where he stood." Dr. Carroll Adams and other faculty I spoke with mentioned the keen awareness Barrus always had of campus affairs and lauded the even manner in which he approached matters of controversy. In his classes, he often spoke of the "golden mean" and, in real life, he lived it.

One measure of a man can be seen in the way he treats those who work for him. Paul Barrus' former secretary and student, Ulna McWorter, who was paid forty cents an hour by the university for her work (the going rate at that time) remembers some amusing incidents from this period: A copy of Grant Wood's painting, *American Gothic*, hung in his office. A student came in to see him one day, noticed the painting, and asked, "Are those your parents, Dr. Barrus?" Another time a different student asked about a picture of Ralph Waldo Emerson which he also had hanging in his office, "Is that you as a young man, Dr. Barrus?" Both incidents greatly amused him, according to McWorter, but without a hint of condescension, he seized the moment to teach, and two students walked away knowing a bit more about early Americana. McWorter considered her boss: "exacting in a kindly manner, and someone with a consistent disposition which made my working conditions very pleasant." They maintained a friendship until his death.

When asked years later if he thought rapid growth of the college was a good idea, Barrus responded, "It's a mixed blessing. When we grow larger as an institution, we lose something. When I came here, each person was an individual. By that, I mean other people took notice of his peculiarities, his idiosyncrasies, his mannerisms. In other words, he was a person."[10]

In those few simple sentences, Barrus reveals a small-town person at heart — not small town in intellect, sophistication, or learning — but at heart. Commerce, Texas, had become his new Winterset, and its people his family.

Times of Change

In the mid-60s, Dr. Gee, anxious to have the school attain university status, asked Paul Barrus to set up the first Ph.D. degree program. Barrus' former student Dr. Ralph Wood, gives some real insight into the dilemma Paul Barrus faced in view of this request when he says in private correspondence with this writer:

> Dr. Barrus had grave reservations about this idea, knowing well that his department was not qualified

to offer a bona fide Ph.D. in English, especially in view of the rigorous requirements he had fulfilled in earning his own degree at Iowa. From what I remember of our conversations about this matter, he was not at all eager to embark upon such a potentially foolish venture. But as always the dutiful and obedient servant, he did what his superiors commanded. When Dr. Gee decided that ET would achieve instant university status by having English offer the first doctorate, Barrus quietly complied.

In his public explanation of how this came about, Dr. Barrus explained it this way: "The news (that is, Dr. Gee's decree that he begin preparations to implement such a program) reached me during a vacation trip to Iowa, and I hurried home to Commerce to draft a syllabus and to confer with my fellow teachers. We were of one mind that quality would be our watchword and tried to compose a curriculum calculated to achieve that objective."[2]

Ph.D. degrees in English were awarded from 1966 through 1971. Dr. Fred Tarpley remembers that during this time Dr. Gee announced that no one without an earned doctorate could be hired. "We lost a great teacher that way. She had a master's degree from the University of Chicago, served as an editor of a series of prestigious textbooks, and she had trained a number of fine high school English teachers."

In 1971 the Coordinating Board of Texas ordered that the Ph.D. be discontinued. Dr. Barrus, always one to see humor in most situations, has said of that decision: "It was rumored that the Board had decided that our faculty in English included no one of sufficient eminence to warrant such an ambitious undertaking. When this reason for abolition became widespread knowledge, one young woman in another department said, 'I'll have the Coordinating Board to know that I've never been eminent with ANYBODY!'"[2]

Although the Ph.D. in English was discontinued, it was replaced with an Ed.D. in the College Teaching of English. Although the requirements changed somewhat for the new degree, it was essentially the same program and since most of the doctoral students were headed for teaching rather than research, it served its purpose well.

Considering the amount of turmoil in much of the United States during the period of racial integration, ET remained remarkably calm. Most of the faculty and students credit Dr. James Gee with making the transition a peaceful one. As Dr. Carroll Adams said of this period, "Largely because of Dr. Gee's leadership, ET was integrated fully and peacefully. 'This is the law of the land, and you will obey it,' he announced in a June 1964 speech to all college employees, and so we did."

Dr. Barrus was solidly behind President Gee when he "announced unequivocally that integration would be 100 percent on the East Texas State College campus." He was not solidly behind some of the other "goings on" of the 1960s. In a listing of things remembered, Barrus included, "The turbulent 1960s when the cry of students' rights camouflaged so-called reform and irresponsible behavior." Of this period he was also heard to say, "This is the first generation that has willingly gone out of its mind." Of this same era, he also said, "After the sixties, people may want a change. If we want to go on demanding, demanding, demanding, and giving nothing in return, it's a one-way street that ends in disaster for the individual and the nation."

A believer in the character-building aspects of self sacrifice, Barrus said: "I believe that anything that doesn't require sacrifice, that doesn't require self-denial, that doesn't demand self-discipline... turns on you and destroys you. I think that's a law of human life."[10]

My favorite Barrus story from this time concerns the young man who wore an outlandish wig to class in anticipation of causing a sensation. Failing to get any reaction from Barrus, he asked, "What do you think of my headdress?" and Barrus replied, "I don't care about your headdress. I'm worried about whether there's anything under it or not."

Another story during this "Do your own thing/anything goes" period which Barrus delighted in telling was of the "fine, conscientious lady teacher with a highly developed moral sensibility who used to buttonhole me in the halls, fix me with a look that made me examine my conscience, and enunciate sternly, 'Dr. Barrus, there's EVIL in the world!' I agreed with her but had no ready recipe for instantly eliminating it."[2]

The Campus Visit of Flannery O'Connor

A Forum Arts program was started in 1959. This gave students an opportunity to hear distinguished speakers such as Senator Lyndon B. Johnson and literary figures such as Pearl Buck, as well as performances by such diverse groups as the Ballet Folklorico of Mexico and the Preservation Hall Jazz Band of New Orleans.

One of Barrus' proudest moments at ET was when Flannery O'Connor came to visit the campus in November of 1962. He had admired her work, and, in his role as director of the Forum Arts program, wanted to invite her to the campus as a speaker. First, however, he thought he should hear her give a presentation. Travel allowances for professors in those days were meager, but it so happened that she was speaking that spring on "The Grotesque in Southern Fiction" at Converse College, and so he traveled by bus, paying his own way, from Commerce to Spartanburg, South Carolina, to hear her speak.

"I was a little startled to see the aluminum crutches, but when she began to speak in her deep Georgia drawl, any idea of her being 'handicapped' vanished," he said. One statement in particular from this O'Connor talk seems to have made a lasting impression on him: "My characters are sometimes criticized for being grotesque," she said, "but in our time it is only in the South that folks are still able to recognize the grotesque."

Determined that ET students *would* hear Flannery O'Connor speak, he mustered up the courage to invite her to Commerce in spite of the fact that his guest speaker budget for the entire year was only $300. "In response to my request, she almost rattled me with her direct, penetrating gaze, but finally I heard her say, 'I'll see about it.'"

In the initial negotiations, he offered her $250 for her appearance, but she replied that she could not afford to leave her work for that amount of money. His second offer of $300 was accepted later when she was also offered an engagement in New Orleans during that same time period. With the extra fee from that added engagement, she agreed to make "a circle" and include Commerce in her itinerary. With that triumph under his belt, he had to face another problem. As he recalled it:

> I remember clearly Dean Sowers' consternation when
> he learned that I had rashly spent all my annual

allowance of $300 to bring her to the campus. My telephone rang, and he said to me, "Paul, do you realize that you've spent ALL your money on this woman? What will you do for the spring program for which your department is responsible?" "Oh," I answered, "that's been taken care of. Ab Abernethy will do a free concert of folk songs as the guest of our folklore teacher."

Dr. Byrd, a close associate of Abernethy, had come to the rescue of Dr. Barrus.

Dr. Fred Tarpley adds some insight to this anecdote about the cost of O'Connor's visit to ET when he says: "Some part of the cost for her appearance was probably paid from the Forum Arts budget since she stayed on campus a few days, and since she spoke in the auditorium at a Forum Arts assembly and in the Home Economics Auditorium as well as in the English classrooms."

Of O'Connor's visit to the campus, Dr. Tarpley recalls that he drove Dr. Barrus to the Dallas airport to pick her up. On their brief tour of the city that day, O'Connor was shown the assassination site of President John F. Kennedy, and she was taken to a house on Turtle Creek painted battleship gray, with a huge Uncle Sam lamp visible in the picture window. The owner, who had been in national news recently, was outside, putting a very large flag in his front yard as they drove by. Both Drs. Barrus and Tarpley remembered that O'Connor commented rather critically on such practices. (In our interview, Tarpley identified the man as General Edwin Walker, a leader of the John Birch Society, a politically active organization at the time of her visit.)

On the way back to Commerce, the men called her attention to the FATE exit sign and they all had a good chuckle. In a volume of O'Connor's letters, Fred Tarpley came across one in which she had written to someone telling of her experience in Commerce, "I was met at the airport by a Christian gentleman." In that same letter, she also mentioned the exit sign to FATE.

Miss O'Connor spent two days on the East Texas campus, "lecturing to a packed auditorium, meeting with individual groups of students, and replying to all questions with her famous honesty and directness.

After a faculty dinner at a local restaurant, someone asked how she had spent the summer, and she replied, 'I did considerable po'ch sittin'."[2]

At a gathering of English students in the Home Economics Building, one student asked, "Miss O'Connor, why do you write?" "In her inimitable Georgia drawl," Barrus reported, "She fixed him with a steady gaze and answered, 'Cause Ah'm kinda good at it.'"

And Miss O'Connor herself told the following story when she was on campus. There was an old lady in California who complained to O'Connor that her book, *A Good Man is Hard to Find,* "left a bad taste in my mouth."

"Ah wrote her," Miss O'Connor commented, "that Ah didn't expect her to eat it." Another one-liner made the ET audience roar when someone asked about the significance of The Misfit's hat. (This is a reference to one of the characters in *A Good Man*...) "The significance of The Misfit's hat is to cover The Misfit's head," she answered.

Dr. Ralph Wood, then an ET student, had this to say about their renowned 1962 visitor and the impact of her words on him in the preface to his own book, *Flannery O'Connor and the Christ-Haunted South*:

> We were well prepared for O'Connor's visit because all the classes in the Hall of Languages had studied *A Good Man is Hard to Find*, her first collection of stories. It would be extremely foolish to suggest that, as a greenhorn English major, I understood them at any great depth, but there is no doubt that they created the chief turning point of my entire academic and religious life. For I saw in her work the integration of two worlds that I had heretofore thought to be not only separate but opposed, even divorced: uproarious comedy and profound Christianity. I had thought that the sour saint was the model of the Christian life, and that somberness was the ultimate sign of serious faith. O'Connor taught me, exactly to the contrary, that the deepest kind of Christianity, as well as the best kind of literature, is finally comic and joyful, glad-spirited and self-satirizing.

Wood also noted that O'Connor had made world-class art from a world he already knew, that of a "supposedly retrograde region and its seemingly small-minded Christianity." This campus visit so inspired him that he continued to study O'Connor (the subject of his master's thesis) and other Catholic writers, so that he, a practicing Baptist, could better understand their perspective.

Dr. Wood, now a renowned O'Connor scholar, is scheduled to be the main speaker at the 2010 Paul Wells Barrus Day event at Texas A&M-Commerce. The title of his proposed topic, "Why East Texas No Longer Belongs to the Bible Belt: '*A Good Man is Hard to Find*'" will, in all likelihood, stimulate new and renewed interest in this writer.

One more thing should be noted about O'Connor's 1962 visit to ET The visiting writer was treated royally in Commerce. She stayed at the home of Professor Balma Taylor, who was later gifted with a plaque from Dr. Barrus bearing these words: FLANNERY O'CONNOR SLEPT HERE.

At the end of her stay in Commerce, O'Connor invited Barrus to visit her at her home in Milledgeville, Georgia. "I did just that," he said.

> She welcomed me warmly, and all that day we sat on the front porch of the home she shared with her mother discussing all manner of things. I don't think the world fully realizes what she was saying. They look upon her stories as horror stories, not realizing that they point out that fatal flaw in every human nature, our inclination to sin. But, she also stresses, in her stories, what she called "*the moment of grace*." In the life of every person, there comes a moment of grace, unexpected sometimes, where one is shown the right way.

This *moment of grace*, of course, is also a theme which runs throughout the Barrus story.

Notes From Inside a Barrus Classroom

As I write, my thoughts return to 1969 when I first met Dr. Barrus. I was then thirty-eight years old, recently widowed with two children to raise, no job prospects, and little confidence in my own ability. I decided to go back to college and continue my education at ET in Commerce, about a thirty-mile drive each way from my home near Sulphur Springs. At registration that fall, he was the only person to come over to where I sat and ask me if he could be of help. Because I was an older student perhaps the others involved in registration thought I knew what I was doing. (Although I had graduated with a B.S. degree from another college in 1951, I hadn't retained very much.)

When I decided to major in English at ET, I had to get permission from Dr. Barrus, department chairman, who turned out to be the gentleman who had helped me at registration. He was very polite, formal, and serious when I went to his office. "Why do you want to major in English?" he asked. I had not thought that out and could only stammer, "Because I like to read." I was thoroughly intimidated by his formal manner and by what I interpreted that day as his dour expression, but I took his suggestion to enroll in his "Development of the English Language" class and another undergraduate English class in American Literature taught by another instructor, in order to prepare for graduate school.

The Barrus class presented the greatest mental challenges I had experienced to that point, and I was inspired to continue as his student. For the first time, I could see clearly how one *should* teach. In this class, I also learned more about world history than I had ever learned in a history class. I learned about *The Oxford English Dictionary* for the first time because of his assignment to study the etymology of a single word of our own choice. I chose "clown," thinking it would be easy and fast, and I still remember the shock upon learning that *The Oxford English Dictionary* was not one, but many books. Seeing so many entries tracing the etymology of one small word made me even more aware of my ignorance and of the distance I had to cover before I could claim to be educated.

Another time, he assigned the memorization of the Lord's Prayer in Old English, and he listened to its recitation by each member of his class. Most of us, I dare say, can still recite it. It's how one of the interviewees for this book and I, although we had never met, greeted each other. When I faltered, she filled in the missing words. I'm sure we both wondered at the time we memorized this prayer in Old English if any possible good could ever come from it. And yet, here we were, many years later, meeting for the first time, connected with Dr. Barrus, with this magical language and with each other. That prayer was the tie that bound us; two streams of consciousness flowed into one as the words came stumbling out in fragments, connecting to sing a hymn of praise in honor of a man who left a lasting impression on both of us.

Notebooks from his classes are the only ones I still have and read. Today I open my notebook from that first class. In my own scrawl, I see his words:

> Watch your language; say what you mean. Words affect what you are. You tend to descend to the level of your vocabulary.... The spoken word is lasting because you can never recall it. When you put ideas into words, you give them immortality. The more words you know, the more life you touch. The more life you touch, the more alive you are.

I came to call these short, pithy expressions, "Barrus Lusters," after an assignment he made to the Emerson class to collect "Emerson Lusters" from his essays and speeches, that is, to select certain passages we found to be interesting and relevant. This next "Barrus Luster," simple and direct, aimed at all of his students, no matter age or intellect, may capture the essence of the man as well as anything he ever wrote: "There are many good things that do not last very long. Awards and trophies eventually are forgotten. Even diplomas will some day merely collect dust. One thing outlasts them all: the love and care you have for human beings. Care endures."

On the first day of my Emerson class, he asked if anyone knew the "perennial and eternal questions all religions have attempted to answer — the same questions asked generation after generation." No one in the class knew the answer, so he must have told us. I see in my notes: "What is man? Who am I? Where did I come from? What am I here for? Where am I going?"

I loved the assignments he gave in that class. He might say, "Take a passage from this essay and write a little essay of your own showing your understanding of that passage." This led to several original pieces I would never have written without prodding: "On Gifts," "On Manners," "On Character," etc. His assignments always gave students room to express their own creativity. He had a very unusual gift for recognizing potential in others when that individual had no inkling of his or her own gift. He could bring out the best in anyone who was willing to try.

In more than one of my Barrus classes, I heard him say, "Life is like a cafeteria line. There are many choices to make, but you can only go through the line one time." (A sobering thought for an eighteen-year-old, and for a thirty-eight-year-old, such as I was at that time, an all-too-uncomfortable truth.)

From the Emerson notebook, I also read, "Both Emerson and Thoreau believed in the latent perfectibility of man." (Although he never said that he didn't believe such, we all knew that he did not, that this was his gleeful irony!) In my notebook for the Mark Twain class, I see "Ralph Waldo Emerson and Mark Twain represent the two halves of the American Soul." By the end of those two classes, we better understood the origin of our own odd mixture of Idealism and Calvinism.

And, in that same notebook, I see a notation I often heard him speak, "Everyone should read the book of Job at least once a year." Although I did not understand why reading the story of Job was important, even after I had dutifully read it as he had instructed us to do, I have since come to understand that it teaches a constructive acceptance of the grief, the sorrows, the troubles of life one can do nothing about.

Recently I have begun to consider another reason he may have had such a profound respect for this particular book. It is probable he saw shades of his own battles with depression in these words of Job: "For the thing which I greatly feared is come upon me, and that which I was afraid of is come unto me. I was not in safety, neither had I rest, neither was I quiet; yet trouble came."

Several times Barrus was heard to say that he had stayed so long at ET because of the native courtesy on the part of the students. Always a great believer in the power of manners, he had a deep appreciation for the politeness of most ET students. And, of course, they treated him with courtesy because he was always most courteous and respectful of students. I remember him as the only professor I knew who consistently stood by the open door of his classroom to greet students by name as they entered. He was always calm, quietly contained, and dressed as if he were about to undertake a formal voyage with his students. And in a sense he was — they were. This was serious business. Most students left their nonsense outside his classroom, but there was always time for a good laugh. For example, Dr. Mark Busby remembers Barrus' comments on the rhythmical nature of language, and in particular, this rhythmical, if ungrammatical, response he claimed he had once heard: "If I'd a knowed I coulda rode, I woulda went."[5]

When it became clear many of us had dreamed or slept through our fourth to eighth grade English grammar lessons, he taught us grammar. I could grasp the concept of past, present, and future tense, but beyond that, I was a lost *noun*. Because he knew vocabulary and grammar so well, he could make people like me understand why a term such as "perfect tense" makes perfect sense. (Perfect tense because it shows perfect action — i.e. action completed.) Another of his students repeated a story he had told her class. It seems a man went into a store and pointed to a wanted object on a shelf. "Is them them?" the clerk asked. Barrus described the sentence as "perfectly imperfect"!

As for one of my favorite personal recollections of being introduced to an unfamiliar word, I remember the day I learned "supercilious" when we came across that word in a line from the Emily Dickinson poem, "I Like to See It Lap the Miles." As he explained that the Latin *super* means *over* or *above*, and that *cilium* means *eyelid*, he raised one eyebrow in a definite arch and cast a downward glance in our direction.

Over the years, I have borrowed from my Barrus notebooks and his teaching techniques time and again. Like so many of his former students who became teachers, I, too, often imitated the master as best I could, though I paled in comparison.

Perhaps no one has written more eloquently of Paul Barrus in the classroom than his former student, Dr. Ralph Wood. In an essay entitled "Literature as a Moral and Spiritual Awakening,"[5] Wood has this to say about Dr. Barrus:

> The paradox of Professor Barrus' influence on me is more drastic than many will be prepared to understand…. Paul Barrus was the first Roman Catholic this Southern Baptist had ever known. I am not exactly sure what I expected to find… But what I found was a difference far beyond celibacy and fasting, rosaries, and novenas. To my grateful astonishment, I discovered in Paul Barrus my moral and spiritual mentor, my father and brother in my own religious

pilgrimage. Little did I then know that this noble teacher would become my lifelong friend.... Our study of fiction and poetry, of drama and the essay, was never an escape from life but always an engagement with the hardest questions and the toughest truths.... Patiently he stood on the shore of knowledge and wisdom, casting forth the lifeline to every sinking soul in the class.... The real teacher, he taught us, is the man or woman who is eager to break the bread of truth with even the rudest beginner.... The one lesson he taught us with unfailing clarity was that there is something fundamentally intractable about the human condition. It cannot be cured by the nostrums of popular psychology and sociology, nor by the myriad self-help books that the columnist George Will calls our "Do-It-Yourself God Kits."

In this same collection of lectures honoring Dr. Barrus, another former student, Dr. Mark Busby, talking about an incident from one of his own classes, says,

After no one could tell me what "obsequious" meant, I caught myself becoming Paul Barrus, as I acted out the meaning of the word just as he had dramatized it to me over twenty years before. "Obsequious," I said, "literally means bowing walking backward," and as I bowed down walking backward I could see clearly in my mind's eye Dr. Barrus doing the same thing.

Dr. Phillip Rutherford, also a former student and essayist, speaks in a humorous tone of meeting Dr. Barrus for the first time in the classroom:

I had never met anyone quite like Dr. Barrus. He did not speak just Standard English — not even Standard Formal Spoken English. He spoke Formal Written English — in complete sentences yet. I could see every comma, every semi-colon, every parenthesis. I could pick out introductory adverbial clauses, underline

prepositional phrases, identify indirect objects. I
could see—actually see—modifying adjectives
descending at a correct 45-degree angle from the
main line of the sentence. I knew if I opened my
mouth an "I seen... " or an "I ain't got no..." or a
"he don't..." would pop out.

One last tribute from *Lectures* concludes my comments on Dr. Barrus
in the classroom. Another of his former students, Jerry Flemmons,
well-known Texas writer and editor, had this to say:

> I was not one of his better students. Unfortunately,
> I was not anyone's better student. But I, perhaps,
> was as much affected by him as any student he may
> have had. Dr. Barrus was a marvelous teacher, but
> you already know that. For someone like me,... shy,
> very unsure of himself, afraid of what might be, of
> what I might become, encountering Dr. Barrus was a
> revelation. He taught me, above all else, that thought
> is precious, that to reason, to think, is possible, if not
> probable. I defy you to find that rare lesson in any
> textbook. It wasn't just that he taught literature, he
> taught the ideas of literature. And as all great teach-
> ers, he had that indefinable ability to make you want
> to learn, to somehow please him. I probably didn't.
> Please him, that is. But he pleased me.

A genuine wonder to his students in the classroom, Paul Barrus
was also held in great esteem by the people he worked with, by his
association with the townspeople of Commerce, by his relatives with
whom he often visited, and he was by no means averse to a good
time. Before continuation of the academic aspects of his career at
ET, let us pause, as he would, for some fun and a good chocolate
dessert with friends.

Friends, Food, and Fun

Several faculty members spoke of the kindness he showed them when they came as strangers to the campus. Charles Linck said this: "He was very accommodating when I first came to the campus from Kansas as a new hire. He got me a room over on Church Street for a couple of nights, and he introduced me to a lot of people around the campus and in town." And Dr. Carroll Adams recalled his first meeting with Barrus:

> I was a brand new professor, just hired at ET as an Economics teacher, just out of graduate school, only thirty years old, when I was introduced to Paul Barrus at the Cadillac Hotel in Greenville. Fred Tarpley had brought him along to our luncheon engagement. I had heard so many wonderful things about Barrus, I hadn't expected to meet such a humble man. Right away I realized, here is someone special, but it took me years to figure out how special. After that first meal we shared, our relationship grew from there. Considering the fact that I was such a young professor just starting out, I was impressed that from the very first meeting, he was always kind to me both personally and professionally. He did not deliver "great words of wisdom," and yet you knew you were hearing great words of wisdom. Also, he was curious about the way other people looked at life.

With their small circle of close friends from the university, these men would often drive from Commerce to the Daisy Sellers Cafeteria in Sulphur Springs for lunch. When Miss Daisy and her helpers saw their favorite customer approaching, they would hustle around to make sure Dr. Barrus was greeted personally and to make certain his favorite foods were set out. He liked Hopkins County Stew, chicken-fried steak, salmon patties, and, of course, Miss Daisy's locally famous desserts.

Paul Barrus is remembered almost as much for his "sweet tooth" as for his more refined qualities. No meal was ever complete for him without dessert—no snack without a sweet. Dr. Bill Tanner, his former student and fellow traveler, tells of the time he and Dr. Barrus were in Corpus Christi to attend a professional meeting of the Conference of College Teachers of English (CCTE) when the older man fell flat on his face as they encountered some steps on their way into the Water Street Café. After he regained his composure, they continued into the café where he celebrated his *"near fall from grace"* with a chocolate-chip cookie and ice cream. His friends always knew when he wanted something sweet because he would peek over his eyeglasses and say, "I'll have one (of whatever) if you will!"

Most often mentioned by his friends was his love of good food. "He knew all the best places. He took me to a 'boarding-house reach' place near the campus where some hungry soul might dump a whole bowl of stuff onto his plate to the disgust of all of us," said Charles Linck, "and sometimes we would go with Dr. Byrd to 'The Holler' to eat the good food prepared by the black ladies there."

Mary Elizabeth Channon, the daughter of his good friends and fellow teachers from this era, Drs. Chester and Ethel Channon, remembers Barrus was a frequent visitor in their home. Although no stranger to East Texas cornbread dressing, he loved what Mary Elizabeth called "Yankee food." Her mother would prepare lamb or turkey with oyster dressing and his favorite white layer cake with chocolate icing when he came to dinner at their home. An ecumenical, Barrus often accompanied her Episcopalian family to concerts, recitals, and church events where her mother and father played cello and violin. Sometimes they would all attend Methodist church suppers together in a nearby segregated black community called Norris, where Barrus always looked forward to the sweet-potato pie they served. This community, referred to above by Dr. Linck as "The Holler" also figures in an anecdote related to me by Vicki Strief, who says her family once visited their cousin in Commerce, and he took them to The Holler to eat. "There I had the best fried chicken I have ever tasted in my life! But, it was also in Commerce that I had another experience I have not forgotten. I had never seen separate facilities for blacks and whites before. I kept asking questions, and my mother kept shushing me."

Paul Barrus was often a favored guest in area private homes, and his hostess always did her best to serve his favorite dishes. In one home it might be leg of lamb; in another, vegetables fresh from the host's garden. Annette Milton and her husband often had her uncle, Dr.

Jim Byrd, and Dr. Barrus as dinner guests in their home. Annette recalls that Barrus requested hot biscuits and fig preserves for dessert when he came for a meal, and he told her that the black-eyed peas she served were cooked "just right—good and done; I don't like my peas to ping in the pot!"

Often he and his friends would drive to Dallas for concerts, theater, or other cultural events. Several of them shared special interests with him. Fred Tarpley mentioned their mutual interest in language. Barrus taught "Development of the English Language" and Latin; Tarpley taught "Dialectology." And, of course, they each taught freshman composition and rhetoric, which first drew them to each other. "He could go from literature to composition to language with equal skill," Tarpley said of his friend. "He had a wonderful personal touch and rapport with people."

Carroll Adams and Paul Barrus shared a love of folk idioms—things and/or ideas expressed in a certain way. "Perhaps," Adams suggests, "because we were from similar kinds of places, we loved expressions like 'The Devil, he got a holt of me.'" (Adams is from a small town in Arkansas.) "Y'all come back now," spoken as an invitation rather than a command, also amused Barrus.

Charles Linck says, matter-of-factly, "Dr. Barrus hired me because I was Roman Catholic, and in addition to my teaching duties at the college, he also put me to work with the Newman Club immediately. I and my then wife did the 'choir,' as she played piano and I sang. We also did some hayrack rides and wiener roasts—Barrus wouldn't ride a hayrack."

I came across Barrus' own account of a winter sleigh ride he had once participated in when he was a young teacher in Iowa which might account for his reluctance in later years to take part in a Texas hayride. The anecdote involved a big horse-drawn sleigh with straw in the bottom, fur robes, and several students—one of whom was a very large, young girl named Dorothy. The rig went around a sharp curve at a good clip. Barrus slipped to the wagon bottom, and Dorothy fell on top of him. After he had dusted himself off, regained his composure, and made sure no one was hurt, it would probably be safe to assume that he had made a silent vow to never ride a horse-drawn conveyance again!

Fred Tarpley's was one of the families adopted by Barrus, or perhaps it would be more accurate to say that they adopted him. However phrased, he became a member of the Tarpley family. He traveled to Mexico with them, visited with them in Hooks, Texas, during school holidays, and sat beside his young friend's mother in the church when Fred was married. Tarpley adds: "Wherever we were, it was understood that he would go to Mass on Sunday. When he visited in Hooks, I would get up early on Sunday morning and drive him to Mass in New Boston because there was no Catholic church in Hooks." All of Barrus' friends seemed to have made this same concession when called upon because they were keenly aware of what his attendance at Mass meant to him.

When asked if he and Barrus spoke in private about religion and religious matters, Carroll Adams said:

> Yes, we talked about religion from time to time but not from the standpoint of controversy or derision. He might say that he didn't understand a particular point of view, but he did not reject it. He was fond of saying, "The church is like a large tree with many branches, and there is room for everyone." At the same time, he was very particular about his own church obligations. If you were away somewhere with him, he would let you know that he needed to attend Mass at a certain time. Once during a casual conversation, I think I shocked him slightly with this statement: "I don't like religious people." "Why, Carroll!" he responded, to which I replied, "Paul, you are not religious. You live your faith, and don't have to talk about it. I see it in your life."

Asked if his friend didn't have some flaws, Tarpley said that he had heard this description of Barrus' frugality: "He so rarely opens his purse, you can hear the hinges creak." Then Tarpley added this caveat: "Yes. He was frugal with himself, but he was generous with other people. And students... no one will ever know how many students he helped along the way. He simply never talked about it."

During the 60s, his cousin Betty and her husband, Phillip Gibson, along with their daughters, Mary Jane and Elizabeth, moved to Richardson, a Dallas suburb. (Betty and Phillip's son, Terry, who was older than the girls, did not move with his family to Richardson.) The other Gibsons were now close enough to visit often with Barrus, the man they always called "Cuz."

Just as Fred Tarpley remembers Paul Barrus as a generous person, so does Mary Jane: "In 1969 I graduated from Richardson High School. I wanted to attend college at ET, but my family had moved to Colorado by this time. Cuz drove up to Colorado to bring me back to Commerce so I could go to college. He opened a checking account for me with a $500 deposit, which I used for college expenses that year. In 1969, that was a great deal of money." He was also sympathetic with her when she clashed with college rules concerning "proper wearing apparel." Mary Jane could make no sense of the rules that maintained girls could not wear pants on campus. "It was very, very cold that winter, and my legs were frozen after walking across the campus from one class to another." She decided not to continue at ET, and returned home to Colorado to attend the University of Northern Colorado where she was joined later by her younger sister, Elizabeth, who thinks it must have been difficult for Mary Jane to be under "his watchful eye" in Commerce.

Elizabeth added that he sent each of them $50 every month when they were students at the University of Northern Colorado and often treated them, along with their parents, to many weekends in mountain retreats. The girls loved to ride horseback, and he gamely accompanied them although riding horses wasn't his idea of having fun.

One incident that happened while they were vacationing together still makes Elizabeth laugh. In the dining hall of the resort they were visiting, there was a particularly sour, grumpy waitress. Cuz started to call her "The Dragon Lady." One day the family gathered there for a meal, but they were too busy visiting with each other to place their orders right away. "The Dragon Lady" approached their table. "Are you here to order, or what?" she asked. Spreading his arms wide in an expansive gesture, Cuz answered, "We are here to CONSUME AND ENJOY!" That rejoinder had, still has, a long life, resurfacing every time the family gathers for a reunion.

Elizabeth also remembers that he helped her write her term papers in college. She would call or write him when she needed advice about how to do a paper, and when her work was returned with a grade of A, she would call to tell him, "WE made an A!" However, even Elizabeth was a little intimidated by her scholarly Cuz. Before she mailed the letters she wrote to him, she would send them to her mother for proofreading and correction!

When the Gibson family lived in Richardson, Barrus often drove from Commerce to visit them. He loved to take Betty and her daughters to North Park Shopping Center, where they always had lunch. Elizabeth says of this treat,

> We ate at a cafeteria in the mall and always sat by the window to watch people walking by. Cuz would give us great descriptions of these people. He would describe some as foreign spies, mysterious persons with secret missions, or people with strange afflictions. When we would ask about a particular person, he might say, "Oh, you don't want to know THAT story."

Of the weekend vacations to which he treated them, Elizabeth says,

> We rarely had a TV or radio in the cabin, so while Cuz read, Mary Jane and I played cards, gradually getting louder and louder as the games progressed and our excitement grew. At that point, Cuz would calmly say we were causing him pain and distress. We would laugh and scream even louder just to get his reaction. He would become more and more dramatic about his discomfort and always end up with his hands to his ears, and laughing along with us.

Mary Jane adds that he was not frugal but very careful with his money. In his later years, he would not take his money out of CDs to invest in stock even though it was paying better returns.

When Paul Barrus became department head at the university, he was remembered to have said to his staff, "The one thing I will not tolerate is the carrying of tales." Aware that he had both spoken and written of the irreparable damage that could be done to another's reputation with gossip, I asked some of his close confidants if he ever joined his friends in gossip, and received conflicting responses: "He loved gossip! He had an indulgence for gossip," said the witty Charles Linck. "No, he didn't gossip," said Fred Tarpley, "He just took a great interest in people."

And often, other people took a great interest in him. Tarpley tells of an incident that took place on one of their visits to Hooks, Texas, when an old gentleman there became fascinated with Barrus: "He got right up close — right in Dr. Barrus' face, and said, 'You still have all of your teeth! Just how old are you?' Without knowing it, the man had hit a raw nerve. Dr. Barrus resented being asked his age."

According to close friends, he came under criticism a few times because some felt he was too protective of faculty members — that perhaps he should have been stricter with certain people or maybe have fired some, but he was so compassionate and sympathetic with others' personal problems, he found that hard to do.

"He had wonderful stories about his students," Fred Tarpley reminisced. "One comes to mind. There was the mother who insisted that her daughter be allowed to take his Ralph Waldo Emerson class although the daughter was a sophomore and the class was for graduate students only. Her reason: the daughter's father's middle name was Waldo." Request refused.

He did not entertain formally in his apartment on Arp Street, but he did have drop-in guests, according to Carroll Adams, who said, "His apartment was furnished with family things from Winterset — like some of his grandmother's finer pieces, and many, many books — well organized, everything in place." Cousin Mary Jane remembers his apartment as more like a townhouse or a condo, "It was near the campus, and he walked back and forth to classes. It was never cluttered, and when I was there, he fed and looked after a cat someone had abandoned."

The friendship shared by Paul Barrus and James Byrd was puzzling to those who saw Byrd, a faculty member, as a rather free spirit, and Barrus, department head, as one more constrained. Both aware of this public perception, they give clues in some of their writings as to what it was that bound them together as friends. In his foreword to *The Paul Barrus Lectures: 1983–1989*, Jim Byrd writes:

> "There are more things in heaven and earth than are dreamt of in your philosophy," Barrus often quoted. One of these mysteries is why I, a friend, even qualified to write this foreword to a book honoring a man who is now a scholarly priest.

Our philosophical differences are legendary.... the antithesis of our religious views have bothered people... (but) since I was teaching Chaucer, I did have 100 questions about the Catholic church. I also admired the fact that St. Joseph's was the only integrated church in Commerce. The fact that the first Mass I attended was the liberation mass in Notre Dame Cathedral during WWII altered my Baptist views somewhat toward tolerance of Catholics.

To the maiden lady who asked, "How could you, Jim Byrd, and Father Barrus be friends all these years?" I said, "After seventy, Barrus became a priest and took the vow of celibacy; after seventy, I'm going to become a radio evangelist and take the vow of avarice. In this world, allow for slight differences among friends. Don't worry; be happy."

In the following whimsical poem about their first meeting and subsequent trip to the little community of Birthright (near Commerce) in order to familiarize Byrd, this new teacher from Alabama, with East Texas, Barrus wrote and recited the following poem at a scholarship dinner for ET students in the Department of Literature and Languages. Says Barrus of the poem, "McNamee dared me to print the verses, perhaps because there was an early prediction in Birthright that I would become a priest, perhaps because of the ironic prediction of my friend becoming a preacher...." The poem quoted below appeared in his "A Moment of Grace" column in *The Commerce Journal*, April 14, 1991:

He arrived in September
And without my prior knowledge
Went straight to the campus
To look over the college.
While there he was told
In tones soft and low,
Dr. Barrus is Catholic!
I thought you should know.
To show him East Texas
In all of its glory

I drove out to Birthright,
And there hangs a story.
At a neat country market
In the shade of an oak,
We paused for refreshment.
We ordered a Coke.
The proprietor eyed us
With quizzical gaze;
Then ventured to question
Our citified ways.
"I figger you a preacher," (addressing Byrd)
And, turning to me,
"You, the old one is learning
Him how it will be."
Well, Jim has not ever
Become priest or preacher,
But, for thirty-five years,
An outstanding teacher.

Although there was always a quiet aura about Barrus, he was not
a shy man. He could laugh at himself and was recognized as an entertainer around the ET campus. He and Dr. McNamee teamed up
to entertain at small gatherings of the English department and once
a year for the whole student body at "Faculty Frolics" with old songs
like "She's Only a Bird in a Gilded Cage." Barrus sang and McNamee
played the violin. They called their act, "Bar Room Ballads," and
they dressed alike in Gay '90s style. Barrus was the waiter, complete
with bow tie, arm garter, serving tray, and a towel draped over his
arm. Dr. McNamee said of Barrus: "He had a good voice range, was
a good singer and entertainer, and he knew ALL of the old, old songs.
He had committed them all to memory."

Barrus once said: "Students, it seems to me, remember me not
for my fulminations against misuse of verb forms but rather for the
pathos of 'She's More to be Pitied than Censured,' 'Oh Frenchie, Oh
Frenchie,' and 'Keep the Home Fires Burning.'"[2] With Dr. McNamee
as his accompanist, and with the good-natured ET students and faculty
in attendance, he had a built-in appreciative audience, primed to see
the dignified, serious professor let down his hair. He also occasionally

teamed up with his good friend and fellow ET professor, Dr. Margaret Wheat, who played the piano while he sang. Dr. Wheat was also one of the friends who often drove with him to dine at the Daisy Sellers Cafeteria in Sulphur Springs.

Another annual campus-wide event Barrus seemed to enjoy was Western Week. He has said of this event: "Western dress, required on pain of fines and possible dunking in a tank set up near the Science Building or incarceration in a makeshift jail, transformed staid lady professors into brash and buxom cowgirls and the male contingent into swaggering cowhands or black-hatted, black-mustached gamblers." To the great delight of students, Barrus mounted a horse, rode around the campus, and posed for photographs. He was no novice to horseback riding because he had sometimes ridden horses with his nieces during summer vacations. Having looked at the lighter side of Paul Barrus, it now appears that more needs to be said about a more somber part of his life.

Dark Night of the Soul

Although there have been brief mentions concerning the depressions he suffered during his stint in the Army, it is now that something more needs to be said about his own dark night of the soul. The terrible mental depressions he suffered over the years call to mind those memorable lines from Dante: "In the middle of the journey of life/I found myself in a dark wood/For I had lost the right path."

Perhaps it was not well-known while he was at ET, but as Dr. Carroll Adams told me,

> Dr. Barrus was prone to depression. He had severe trials of faith, and he was convinced that he was going blind. The two were connected in some way. He would get into a very dark state—not able to function. When this came upon him, he would withdraw into a shell. Not his friends—not even his doctor or medicines could get him to do anything about these bouts with depression. He refused to talk to a mental health professional because he felt it was something he had to work through himself. He was convinced that it was a spiritual, not a physical or medical condition.

Sometimes he could be teased into a better mood. After a visit with him one afternoon Adams said goodbye, and Barrus replied: "I may not be here when you get back. I want to go to sleep and wake up in God's presence," to which Adams responded, "Then I'll meet you in the pavilion of the saints!" During one particularly bad spell, Adams went over to Barrus' apartment and said to him, "*Get your lazy ass out of that bed and do something about it!*" He got right up according to his friend.

Dr. Ralph Wood sheds light on this reference to Barrus' "severe trials of faith which he considered a spiritual condition" in this excerpt from the moving tribute to his old professor after his death:

> The God of Paul Barrus' faith—the one and only true God—is the God who took the form of suffering flesh at Bethlehem, who made his prayers and supplications with tears wherever he went, and who

died with a loud cry at Golgotha. Paul Barrus was indeed a godly man, a man unashamed to confess his own doubts and fears. He underwent a profound crisis of faith in his early sixties when, as he confessed to me and to others, he came to doubt not only whether God is good, but also whether God even exists. Again, in his seventies, when he was almost blinded by cataracts, he doubted that his life had further meaning or use. And, until the very end, he admitted his dread of dying.

Knowing he still had bouts of depression after he had become a priest, and especially as he grew very old and his fear of dying grew more pronounced, one might well reflect on the possible root cause(s) for this despondency in such a good man who had a rewarding career in two professions, was much admired, and lived to an old age.

The "moment of grace" mentioned earlier in the O'Connor section comes when the character is in great inner turmoil and struggle with himself. I think of this, and I am drawn back to the 1943 letter Barrus wrote from Camp Callan in a state of despair. In the letter, he spoke of "my Gethsemane," and "the silent anguish in my heart that finally left me dazed and almost inert." I believe that out of this particular dark struggle arose at least one of Paul Barrus' moments of grace.

The Ideal Professor

His depressive bouts did not diminish his standing as "The Ideal Professor" although he would undoubtedly dispute that label. As Dr. Carroll Adams expressed it, he "was a man of total humility—spiritual and intellectual. It was something you didn't always know until you got to know him well." But it was as an ideal professor that others came to look upon him long before he retired from college teaching, and it is one that has lived on long after his demise.

This man was, by all accounts, totally prepared for every class he ever taught from the first little rural grade school in Iowa to university classes. He liked to tell this anecdote about visiting high school English classes as an outreach effort on behalf of ET in surrounding small East Texas towns:

> We received a warm welcome, but the public school
> teachers sometimes followed the admonition,
> "Physician, heal thyself." Many a time, I'd just settled
> myself in a high-school English class when the in-
> structor would smilingly say, "Boys and girls, this is
> Dr. Barrus. I'm sure it will be a treat if he teaches the
> poem we have assigned for today." And so I would
> rise, smilingly, gather my scattered thoughts, and
> discourse on perhaps "Ode on a Grecian Urn" or
> Edna St. Vincent Millay's "Renascence."[2]

It is possible that high school teachers *did* want to put him on the
spot, but it seems more likely they did not realize the effort he put forth
in his preparation of even the simplest poem for class presentation.

"Everyone thought he was a great scholar, although no one ever
saw him in the library. The rest of us would go to the library to see
what one or more of the new critics had to say about the work under
discussion so that we would know what to say about it. He chose to
read the original, over and over," Dr. Linck said of Barrus' method
of preparation for his classes. Linck liked to tease him about his
disregard for the latest fad in literary criticism: "Have you taught
the new Mark Twain?" "Hadn't thought about it," Dr. Barrus would
respond. From my own experience in his classes, I do know that he
sometimes assigned readings in literary criticism. We soon learned,
though, that what he wanted us to take away from such readings was
not to parrot what the critic thought about a primary work but to
learn to think for ourselves.

Early on, he showed great interest in helping ET become a first-rate
school. As the sponsor of Kappa Delta Pi, the honorary fraternity
in education, he enlisted the help of an able assistant, student Fred
Tarpley, a junior English major, to help arrange the first Honors Day
program in April 1954. Out of this alliance grew the Forum Arts
program discussed earlier.

Not one to follow trends which he thought unacceptable, Paul
Barrus refused to go along at a time when the National Council of
Teachers of English was promoting what they called "students right
to their own language." According to Dr. Tarpley, "They were ad-
vocating that writing teachers allow their students to submit college

compositions written in the students' home dialect." This was at a time when the quality of student writing was already eroding. Around ET, Paul Barrus became known as a great defender of Standard English when, in a speech to Kappa Delta Pi on April 30, 1975, he said he had become completely baffled

> upon reading the solemn declaration of the guardians
> of our mother tongue (a satiric reference to NCTE)
> that a norm for clear, lucid, precise, and graceful
> expression was plainly elitist, undemocratic, snob-
> bish, and downright bigoted. This scholarly conclave
> further avowed that every person has what it called
> a "right" to communicate in his own unique dialect,
> whether it be the esoteric vocabulary of so-called

> "jive" talk, the four-letter words of much contemporary publication, the gobbledygook of officialdom, and certain presumably scholarly meditations or the staccato reports of news commentators. Don't they all communicate?
>
> Ah, there's the rub! Communication through speech, gesture, and writing, all will admit, is the chief mark of distinction between man and what are called the "lower species," and yet, in accepting this truism the psychology of language, its infinite capacity for lasting good or ill — is blithely overlooked. How we communicate is as important, if not more significant, than WHAT we communicate.

His steadfast dedication to and interest in excellence for ET is reflected in this statement, "It is my belief that unless a college or university education provides a student with a furnished mind — that is, inner resources — then it has been a failure. By inner resources, I mean the capacity to find fulfillment in the world of ideas."

Preparation for his classes was always foremost in his mind. Preparation, of course, entails organization, and he demanded that his students be organized and prepared for class as well. Somehow, though, there was always class time for spontaneity; always time to savor a humorous moment, and to take full advantage of a "teachable moment."

In preparation for this remembrance of him, I found myself arguing passionately with someone who maintained that Barrus had taught theology in his courses at ET. I turn again to Dr. Ralph Wood, who had far more classroom experience with Dr. Barrus than I, for support: "... This is not for a moment to suggest that Dr. Barrus ever turned the lectern into a pulpit. He understood, ever so clearly, the difference between preaching and teaching, between proclaiming the way of salvation and explaining the way of all flesh." To this keen observation, I would add this: Paul Barrus was a well-instructed and devoted Catholic, and he could have recited the views of the best known theologians, but he had better ways to teach us. Paul Barrus had great respect for all his students — for those who could appreciate ideas presented by such lofty thinkers as, say, Milton or Emerson, and equal respect for those who were more talented in other "practical" ways. It should come as no surprise, then, that so many did consider him the ideal professor.

Those unfamiliar with his writing may not know just how accomplished he was at that, also. He wrote newspaper columns for awhile, as well as occasional book reviews and short stories, interesting journals and diaries, and extraordinarily beautiful letters.

Paul Wells Barrus, Writer

Throughout this story I have quoted from Barrus' "A Moment of Grace" columns in *The Commerce Journal*. In these columns, started in 1991 when Jim Byrd learned that the local newspaper needed a clergyman to contribute to the Religion Page on each Wednesday, he convinced Barrus, already in Grand Prairie at Immaculate Conception Church, to take the job. Dr. Byrd, who was, at that time, writing a Sunday column for the newspaper, acted as Barrus' agent in Commerce, always making sure that the Barrus' columns got to the Commerce editor on time. In a departure from the customary topics of his columns such as growing up in Winterset or life as a teacher, friend and priest, he wrote a book review of Robert J. Waller's *The Bridges of Madison County* for *The Commerce Journal* in 1993. Barrus introduces this piece by reminding his readers he had once taught in a one-room country school known as Lone Star, fourteen miles southwest of Winterset, when he was seventeen years old:

> Occasionally I walked home in the interests of my grandparents, who were not well. When the weekend visits drew to a close, my great uncle Tom would hitch his horse to a buggy and drive me seven miles west of town, and I would walk the remaining seven miles to my boarding place with Mr. and Mrs. Wes Evans. My path extended straight south through the Roseman Covered Bridge. This bridge is featured in the book, *The Bridges of Madison County*, still a bestseller.
>
> I have just finished reading this book, and, of course, enjoyed the references to familiar places — Hogback and Cedar Covered bridges, the town of Winterset, and Iowa Highways 169 and 92. The book itself, though, leaves me baffled.

Barrus offers a brief plot summary and then a touch of irony as he says of the male protagonist:

> He remains in the vicinity for four days, during which he and Francesca, the farmwife, conceive a burning passion for each other. They go to bed together, and there follow pages of detailed presentations of various positions of sexual coupling. These descriptions with the jargon of professional photography sometimes make for tedious reading.
>
> The irresistible photographer in the story is a creature of another world, having remained at a now dead Darwinian "stem" when life could be a poetic dream and indiscriminate cohabitation with a "soul mate" its apotheosis. The farmwife wishes to fly away with the super-lover, but says that her sense of "responsibility" precludes further bliss.

What follows is a true, although truncated, reflection of Barrus thinking and philosophy: "To me, the book is an oversimplification of this brief and complicated adventure into consciousness that we call human life.... And then, quite playfully, he ends the review with a limerick referring to his long-time colleague at ET, Jim Byrd:

> I once knew a teacher named Jim,
> Who instructed with vigor and vim.
> He saw through baloney
> And attitudes phony
> And his view of this book was quite dim.

All that is not to say Barrus was unaware of the charms of Madison County's covered bridges. In one of his earlier newspaper columns, he devoted the entire space to the reprint of a letter written by a retired Iowa educator, Mary Jane Pray, to their hometown newspaper. In part, he quotes Ms. Pray as saying of those same bridges:

> ... In getting back to the reason for the weekend festival in October, the very first covered bridge (known as the Holliwell Bridge) was built in the fall of 1854 across the Middle River.... Madison County paid John McCartney $500 to build it. The bridge had

a 40-foot span with a framed approach at each end of it. The timbers were hewn 16 inches square and stringers of the main span measured 44 feet long.... The bridges of Madison County are now sometimes called the "Kissing Bridges."

Madison County covered bridge

PWB as short story writer: In "Fragments of Experience," a short section of *Levels of Consciousness*[3], Barrus writes fiction based on actual experiences he observed growing up in Winterset. In "Bitchie," the narrator tells of the little dog that lived with Lutie down on Gospel Ridge, the rough side of town: "Once Lutie had come tramping through the woods right past Ten-Foot where a lot of boys from town were swimming. When we saw her coming, we dived in, but Lutie laughed and called out, 'You ain't got no surprises for me.'" Next, the narrator reveals a sympathetic Lutie trying hard to find a home for some of Bitchie's puppies. After she fails to do so, and the dog catcher comes to carry them away, we see Lutie crying, and hear her say, "Poor little Bitchie, they'll shoot her and all her pups dead. She only done what lotsa folks in this stuck-up town does all the time. But Bitchie couldn't get by with it."

Then there's the short, tender story of the old couple who fell in love at the Old Folks' Home. When she died, no one bothered to tell him. Soon he was sitting alone in their usual place—the love seat against the east wall of the Home—confiding to anyone who would listen, "I've lost my girl. Her name was Dolly. They didn't let me know. An' they buried her 'way off in Ohio."

This next story reveals Barrus' appreciation of humor. It is titled, "Other People's Money," and the narrator tells of Mr. Swenson, a Lutheran, dedicated to serving his church. It was his job to collect and count the donated money. One Sunday during the depression, he collected $300. Because the amount was so large, he was nervous about being robbed, and he asked another man to accompany him to the bank to deposit the money. The next day he was called by the church treasurer, who asked him what happened to the money he was supposed to deposit. "What do ya mean wha'd I DO with it? I took it right to the bank an' dropped it in. THAT's what I done with it. Matt Weaver was with me an' saw me do it!" When the money was finally found at the bank, the treasurer tried to apologize, but Mr. Swenson had had enough. The narrator then asked him, "Mr. Swenson, did this experience turn you against the Church? Did you continue attending services there?" "Why, sure I kep' on," he replied, "The Church is bigger than any of the numbskulls the good Lord has to depend on to run it."

All of Paul Barrus' stories are very human, and almost all end with moral tags. They reveal his keen insight into the follies, failures, and triumphs of human nature—as well as his own love, sympathy, and respect for his fellow man. And above all, they reveal his quiet sense of humor.

PWB as letter writer, extraordinaire: From a short piece Paul Barrus wrote in 1990 (unpublished, as far as I could determine) one can see the value he placed on the almost lost art of letter writing and understand why he became such a prolific practitioner of this art:

> Letter writing is essentially a civilizing practice in a world more and more addicted to insincerity, self-gratification, and narcissism.... In our preoccupation with self, our conversation is often banal and superficial. Our impoverished vocabulary and, with the passing years, our decreasing physical activity find us cynical. Let us forestall this bleak prospect of the future by sitting quietly, searching for the

exact conveyance of our joys, our regard for friends and the communion of thought and feeling which is our uniquely human prerogative.

The other day I read a letter written when I was six years old to my aunt telling of the arrival of my brother, who is now in his 70s. Like magic, I was transported to early childhood and for a little while I became a little boy. I returned to this present day with its problems and responsibilities refreshed. Boxes of letters line my shelves, each bearing the flavor, the unparalleled personality of those who have touched my life.

I cannot spare a single friend—those who are still with me and those who are gone. To bring them into my study, I merely read their letters, some written 50 or more years ago.... Letters have a kind of immortality. Let us carry them close to our hearts.

Where are those letters today? Fortunately his family, recognizing their importance as a familial as well as a historical document of the era, has preserved them—several hundreds of letters tied in neat bundles—bearing 1-, -2, and 3-cent stamps. Reading the letters, one can see not only into the lives of his friends but more importantly into the life of Barrus and the era in which he lived. It doesn't take much imagination to realize that for every letter he received, he had written one in return. As mentioned earlier in the introduction to this book, Dr. Ralph Wood and a few other friends donated many of the letters they had received from him over the years to the Barrus archives at ET. Unfortunately, more folks have not done so.

In typical Barrus style, he continued to write meticulous accounts of travels down through the years, recording mileage, expenses, and observations. The following is excerpted from a letter to a friend concerning a trip he took alone from Commerce to Des Moines in August/September of 1952:

> ... Then about 10:20 o'clock, I set out for Ottumwa for what I hoped was to be the final chapter in the settling of Cousin Dora Mann's estate. The day was the sort which I have enjoyed only in Iowa in early

autumn. The Studebaker purred down the highway with a smoothness and ease of operation utterly different from the antics of the Chevrolet.…At Pella, the Dutch town, I stopped to mail some postcards and to have a snack—Pella bologna sandwich and coffee—at the spic and span Garden Café. There was a lively crowd in the restaurant; the Dutch features were unmistakable.…The little white buildings, situated in groves of tall trees or on a pleasant knoll, have the same appeal for me that they did thirty-three years ago this fall when, at seventeen, I was a teacher of Walnut #3 in Madison County, Iowa. The children playing in the schoolyard, the American flag rippling in the September breeze, the great fields of corn on every side—how can I say what these mean to me? In our worship of numbers and of bigness we are fast eliminating these little citadels of individualism in an age when mass mindedness seems to characterize all our thinking.…

Carrying letters close to his heart is what he did for almost ninety years—not only letters he had received but some of those he had carefully handwritten or laboriously typed on an old-fashioned typewriter, on stationery imprinted with his favorite Bible verse from Sirach, 6:14: "*A faithful friend is a sturdy shelter; he who finds one finds a treasure.*" More excerpts from Barrus' own letters can be found in Part IV (Immaculate Conception Parish chapter) and in the Appendix to this book.

A Man Who Came to Teach and Left as Legend

Recently, I mentioned to a former ET student that I was writing Dr. Barrus' story and asked him if he had known Barrus. "No, I didn't know him personally—I wasn't at ET during his era—but I know him!—everybody I know knows him. He is larger than life. Paul Barrus is a legend."

How he became a legend springs from his philosophy of teaching—one he put into practice every day of his long teaching life.

He was a great teacher because he devoted his life to it. He saw this profession as a calling, more important than anything else in his life. As he has expressed it: "I think unless a person has a definite calling to teach, he shouldn't teach. I never stepped across the threshold of the classroom in all of those years I taught without experiencing a thrill. Every class period was a new experience."

He stood up for people whom others did not see possibilities in, and he challenged each person to live up to his expectations of them. When I was a doctoral student at the university and had applied for a teaching position as an intern, another professor stopped me on campus to tell me that Dr. Barrus had come strongly to my defense when another member of the selection committee had tried to block my appointment. I did receive the appointment, and later I went on to have twenty good years as a teacher at Richland College in Dallas before I retired. Because he had once seen the possibility in me when others could not, I was challenged, constantly, to live up to his expectations even when he was no longer a presence in my life.

His moderation and even-tempered approach to most matters was marveled at by students and faculty alike. The college yearbook of 1959 was dedicated to him with these words of praise:

> Because your job on this campus is, perhaps, the most difficult of all jobs, that of teaching students their own language; Because you have built a reputation for scholarly classes and the highest ideal of academic achievement;… a model for the ideal type.… Because from year to year, you have demonstrated the real quality of greatness by briefly dropping to our level and entertaining with comedy and song; We, the staff of the 1959 LOCUST, respectfully dedicate this issue as a measure of appreciation for your outstanding work on this campus.

Paul Barrus often said that he had stayed so long at ET because of the native courtesy of the students:

> Students were courteous enough in the North, but they have something different here. I had only one student in all of my twenty-six active years here

who even approached rudeness. And so I thought I'd better stay. He was angry about a grade, and he came storming into my office and ranted, really ranted. Finally he ran out of steam, and I said, "Mr. So-and-so, to carry on a discussion in your present frame of mind would be futile. Come back when you can talk rationally." He turned on his heel and left. I was disturbed, of course. Then in about a half hour, here he came. He apologized. I said, "Well, good. Now we can talk it over." That's the only case I ever had.[3]

All college teachers will recognize that if this is the only case of student rudeness he encountered in twenty-six years of teaching, he was, indeed, a disarming and inspired teacher, with a good deal of magic dust sprinkled in, to boot.

Paul Barrus did leave his beloved ET for another way of life and another profession. But, in heart, a part of him remained there, as he often said. One reason for this is that the people who loved him would not let him go. He was often invited back to the campus as a guest lecturer long after his retirement from college teaching.

༄

PART IV

A Happy Return to Texas
and Parish Work

A Surprising Turn of Events Leads Back to Commerce

IT IS NOW SUMMER, 1982. Paul Barrus had remained at the retirement home run by the Sisters of Mercy where he continued: observing, learning, serving for about two and a half years under the shadow of the prediction made by the Texas physician who had operated on his eyes shortly before he left Commerce that he would soon be blind. He had never given up on the belief that he could be more useful if his eyesight could be improved. Some months into his stay there, he met a Des Moines eye surgeon who said to him, "I think I can fix that eye problem." *And he did*!

Often invited back to Commerce to be honored at various university events, he had returned before for short visits when he was able to do so. Now, with greatly improved eyesight thanks to the Iowa surgeon, he returned to Commerce for what he thought would be an extended visit, with every intention of returning home to Des Moines and the Sisters of Mercy when his Texas visit ended.

He registered at a hotel in Commerce. In his absence, Father Henry Petter had become the new pastor at St. Joseph's. When the young priest heard that his friend was back in town, he called to invite the older man to stay at the rectory and take charge of St. Joseph parish while he was away for an extended period on church business. Surely, no more welcoming words could have been spoken, and the offer was immediately accepted.When Father Henry returned, he was so impressed with the way Barrus had taken over, and with what grace he had worked with the parishioners, that he asked him to stay on indefinitely as associate pastor. "How long will you be here," Father Paul asked, and his young friend answered, "The Bishop says that I will be here for about three more years." "Fine then, I shall come back," Barrus responded, and he left immediately for Des Moines, staying only long enough to say good-bye to the Sisters and to gather his possessions for the move to the rectory at Commerce. Barrus' fear he would not be useful as he aged would remain an unfounded one.

Although neither man could have known how their relationship would grow and bear fruit through the years, this was the beginning of a commitment to each other and to God that would last for almost two decades, giving them the opportunity to serve in four different parishes, and most importantly, giving the older man another chance to fulfill his lifelong desire of being an active Roman Catholic parish priest. This was the church where he had served happily as both deacon and priest until he went to live in Des Moines. This was where he wanted to be.

<h2 style="text-align:center">Welcomed Back
to St. Joseph Catholic Church
in Commerce</h2>

Father Paul's return to Commerce is remembered clearly by Theresa Hooker Petter (future sister-in-law of Father Henry) in these words:

> I met Father Paul in 1982 during my second year at ETSU. Like other teens I knew, I had just left home for college in the Fall of 1981. I was happy to be away from home for the first time; away from a family of seven children and away from my Catholic church and its conservative style. It didn't take long for me to fall in love with the small town church, St. Joseph, and its parishioners. The elderly ones invited students like me to lunch on Sunday and told us to bring our laundry!
> My still conservative nature was rattled, however,

when Father Henry Petter, the new pastor, began to offer mass out of the rectory! He also sang, played the harmonica, the guitar, and wore longish hair! Before long, Father Paul came to live at the rectory. I was pleased because I felt that he would be the conservative balance to Father Henry's less conventional style.

Father Henry and Father Paul, 1995.

Next, Theresa gives some wonderful insight into the relationship between the two priests—the youthful Henry and the older Paul—in which one can almost see Father Paul shedding some years, even as one does *not* see Father Henry putting down his guitar, or becoming "conventional."

Father Paul's ageless sense of humor quickly appeared during our Tuesday night Newman Club Mass and meetings held regularly in the rectory. (Newman Clubs are Catholic student organizations.) As soon as Mass would end, he and Father Henry took us to the kitchen, opened the cupboards, and let the students help themselves to snacks. Soon, they were part of our group. They sang with us, talked with us, and participated in our events.... We grew from the original seven to more than forty members. An average meeting had close to thirty in attendance.

This friendship between the young Theresa and the octogenarian grew:

We began running errands together. I would drive his car to Braums to buy his favorite vanilla sundae with chocolate topping and whipped cream with no nuts. We'd drive to Sulphur Springs to have lunch at the old Sellers Cafeteria. I took him to visit his close friend/colleague Professor Jim Byrd, and we would drive to Greenville to appointments of various kinds. Some of the best times we had were in his kitchen. He would don an apron, wash dishes, or pick up a tray and begin to belt out a tune like "She's More to be Pitied Than Censured." We would make homemade blackberry cobbler, and sometimes we would sit and laugh with Dollie, the cook, as she prepared supper and complained about her relatives. I learned to make his favorite dish — salmon patties with mashed potatoes and English peas, then a white cake with chocolate icing for dessert. He was in heaven!

When this same Newman Club, with Theresa as president, went on a retreat to Telephone, Texas, the members took black and white baseball t-shirts with club emblems and sewed small white squares on the collar for Father Paul and Father Henry, both of whom wore them quite happily, she remembered. "They both connected with every member on such a deep level that most of us became much more deeply committed to our faith." She and her friends were privy to a side of Father Paul not shown to everyone. To their great delight, he would read their palms and predict their futures, as well as read their daily horoscopes aloud.

Barrus' cousin, Elizabeth, sheds even more light on this side of Paul Barrus:

> Mom used to say he would entertain at family gatherings by reading palms and telling fortunes. Sometimes he would look at a palm and then look up in horror, close the palm, and walk away, always with a smile. When I was about eighteen, he "read" my palm, and then walked away saying he just couldn't tell me what he saw. I always wondered if he was really kidding."

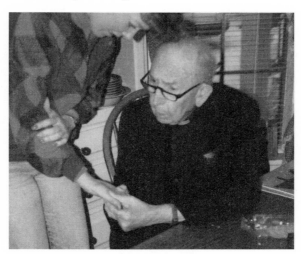

Father Paul plays at palmistry

Theresa also reports that Father Paul was not above poking good-natured fun at himself and other clergy. She remembers that he dressed up on Halloween night as "Sister Disciplina" to entertain the Newman Club and others. In particular, she was impressed with his clever way of making up short, catchy sentences from the letters on his friends' license plates. For example, the letters of his own plate were "JWK," so he referred to it as "Jump Wide, Kiddo." Theresa's license plate letters, "ZJH," became "Zebras Jump High." Another example of Barrus' playful nature can be seen in this telephone message he typed and left for Father Henry:

> Wednesday, 6:10 p.m.
>
> After ten thirty tonight please call Father Tom.
>
> It may be late
>
> And after a meeting
>
> But Father Tom
>
> Will await your greeting.
>
> He's eager soon
>
> To begin his labors
>
> And said he was glad
>
> That we will be neighbors.

Father Henry recalls that he and Father Paul worked well together at St. Joseph in Commerce until something completely unexpected occurred, as he describes here:

> Father Paul was happily taking on more and more duties, and I was ready to get credentials to teach a class at the University when suddenly, in the spring of 1983, I was transferred to Immaculate Conception Church in Grand Prairie. This was an unexpected assignment. I had been told that I would be in Commerce for three years, and Father Paul took on the assignment as assistant pastor because he expected me to be there. When I received my new assignment, I asked him to stay on in Commerce with the new pastor who was appointed to replace me.
>
> When I came back from Grand Prairie for a visit with him, I could see that he and the new pastor didn't mesh, and that Father Paul was making plans to move back to Iowa. "This is not going to work," he told me.

Paul Barrus had influenced for the better more than two generations of people. Now we can see the influence of Father Henry on him. Henry's youthful spirit had helped to rejuvenate the older priest, had given him purpose, a sense of belonging, and the opportunity to be useful. Now, it *appeared* that window of opportunity was closing once more.

"Wait! Don't move yet," Henry told him, "Let me see if I can work out something." He got permission from the bishop to move Father Paul to Immaculate Conception parish as his assistant. Of this experience, Father Henry says, "It was not difficult to get permission to take Father Paul along to the next assignment since they saw me as taking care of him. Little did they know how much he was doing for me, and for the parish."

It took some time, however, to make all of the arrangements for the move. Father Henry had to make plans, then find and hire workers to make a comfortable study/bedroom apartment for Father Paul in the rectory at Grand Prairie. They moved him there in June of 1984. It was a good move and a good match.

A Grand Experience in Grand Prairie: Immaculate Conception Parish

As he settled into Grand Prairie, Texas, the home of his second assigned parish, Father Paul was still able to get around quite well. In addition to his duties as associate pastor of Immaculate Conception Catholic Church, he was invited to teach an honors English class of a dozen children—all talented and gifted eighth-grade students at Immaculate Conception School. Dr. Diane Cooper, principal of the school, explains in a letter to me:

> When Father Paul came to live in the rectory at Immaculate Conception Church, it was immediately evident that he had two great talents: one was as a teacher, and one was as an expert in language and literature. It was also clearly evident to me as principal that this was a rich and powerful resource that we could tap to the benefit of the students. One of my concerns was that our gifted students were not being challenged as fully as I wanted. In Father Paul, we found the perfect match of person, position, and talents. He conducted their class as an enrichment seminar. They discussed words and

their meanings, etymologies, nuances, applications, derivations, and the like.

He brought to them the breadth of his knowledge in the classics, in philosophy, in music, and in art. In his seminar, he was unquestionably the leader and they the followers. He used to perfection the Socratic techniques and opened up young minds to the excitement and the richness of culture beyond that of modern American youth culture. He taught his students the best of what it meant to have a life of the mind. He refused to tolerate sloppy thinking, sloppy writing, and superficial reading.

(Paul Barrus had used almost the same words many years earlier to describe Lewis Worthington Smith, his favorite professor at Drake, when he said: "He had an absolute intolerance of sloppy thinking and sloppy writing.")

In her letter, Dr. Cooper continues:

Mostly he talked, questioned, probed — and students answered, listened, wrote, and learned. It was amazing to watch. I used to try to sneak into his classes on occasion, just to listen. I always learned something new. For the 12- and 13-year-old-kids he taught, he might as well have been from Mars. But they learned and they absorbed his love of the intellectual life.

He became very much a part of the faculty…. He was a warm, engaged, and engaging colleague…. He was a man out of his time in many ways, but he gave us all a look into a world which actually may have been better, though less modern and less convenient.

He was so well-liked by the students of this class that he was asked to continue as the teacher for the talented and gifted for several more years. In a letter to Ralph Wood, he said of this once-a-week class: "This year, our literature selection will begin with mythology, and in addition, there will be vocabulary building, functional grammar, composition and spelling."

It is easy to see that those students had no free ride, nor did anther class of which he said, in this letter to Wood: "We are accompanying Ulysses on his circuitous travels home to Ithaca, and our next reading will be Twain's *Pudd'nhead Wilson*." In yet another letter, he says, "These pupils like to learn proverbs from German, and they like couplets, too, each of which carries a lesson." To illustrate this point, he quotes two couplets he teaches, such as these two rhymes: "Between you and I/Makes me cry," and "To say, 'have saw'/Is against the law." In this same vein, he continues:

> This morning I said to them, "I'm determined that you learn to use the variousforms of 'lie' and 'lay' correctly, and if you do, you will know something that many college graduates do not know." Then, assuming a monitory mien, I solemnly announced that anyone who failed to discriminate correctly between "affect" and "effect" would be banished to outer darkness on finishing the course.

After a class trip to San Antonio, one of his students presented him with a gift, saying, "This is a present from Mark and I." He thanked her and said with a grin, "I am happy to thank you for your thoughtfulness, but before I accept the gift, please correct your usage. And tell me why." She did, much to his happiness, he reported. (He doesn't say whether this student ever gave him another gift, but he gave her one she will not likely forget.)

Upon discovering that these exceptionally bright students had only a vague idea of the location of various states, he told Wood,

> I decided to teach place geography, which has long ago been discarded to make room for "problem solving" and "life adjustment." I revived the old-fashioned practice of "bounding" in which I was drilled in grade school. They learned, for example, that Iowa is bounded on the north by Minnesota, on the east by Illinois and Wisconsin, on the south by Missouri, and on the west by Nebraska and South Dakota. This procedure was repeated for all the states.

This little story reminded me that part of the Barrus magic was his willingness to meet students (no matter how young or old) where they were at that moment, and to devise a method by which they could rise to where he wanted them to be, all without any hint of condescension. His successful tenure at Immaculate Conception School was not one-sided. As Dr. Cooper explains:

> He loved being with us. He became energized just walking into the classroom. Years fell away as he sat at his desk with his students around him. He looked visibly younger while he taught, so I think the sheer joy of teaching kept him vibrant and alive for years longer than might have been without the stimulation and fun.

Father Paul continued to have close contact with those students as they grew up. According to Father Henry, "He was still advising them in later years as they wrote admission requests to various colleges." One of these students, Michael Nasky, pretty well sums up what many of these former eighth graders feel concerning their unusual teacher and this unusual experience, when he says, "I learned more about more subjects in that one class than I did in all the rest of my studies combined.... He opened my eyes to poetry, Shakespeare, and introspection, among many other things."

Cathy Hare was an out-of-the-ordinary student when she came to Father Paul at the Immaculate Conception Rectory for private instruction to prepare her for the Graduate Record Exam. (At the time, a recent papal encyclical had just granted women the right to study in seminary, and although Cathy was anxious to begin, she feared that she would not do well on the language sections of the GRE.) Of her study with him, Cathy says:

> Father Paul could teach students of any age. Whether in an eighth-grade classroom, delivering a homily, or teaching a 42-year-old how to take the GRE, Fr. Paul modeled his approach on that of Jesus. He taught through analogy. It has been almost 20 years since I would drive out to Grand Prairie with my workbooks in hand. Undaunted, Father Paul would

take me through each exercise, showing me how the differences between things often pointed to their similarities. With his patience and intelligence he enabled me to pass the GRE, and as a result, I was accepted to the seminary, earned advanced degrees in theology, even studying for two years in Rome.

Paul Barrus was not one who agitated for change in the Catholic Church, but when it came as a result of Vatican II, he accepted it with good grace, for the most part. Shortly after women were accepted into seminary, here he was helping a woman to prepare for future study there. It is hard to imagine, though, that he would have been that supportive had she been preparing for the priesthood. He was, after all, a great believer in tradition.

Not all was study in the time she shared with him, as Cathy explains:

> We would often go out to lunch with Father Henry. One of Father Paul's favorite lunch places was the old Highland Park Cafeteria on Knox Street. From our first "date," it was clear that Father Paul liked to dress up, adding a little dash to his clerical suit. Being appropriately dressed to him meant the wearing of a hat. He had an old Panama Straw that he favored in the spring and summer. I would wear one of my old-fashioned straws and "gussy" it up with silk flowers to match my dress. Slacks were not an option when a lady dined with Father Paul.

Paul Barrus had a genuine appreciation for a well-dressed woman. He had a special fondness for beautiful hats, and he was not too shy to tell a woman that he liked her dress. He did not like earrings, however, according to a short essay in his own handwriting I found among his papers. He considered the wearing of earrings, "barbaric."

It was at Immaculate Conception Parish that he became well-known for his homilies. Father Henry and others spoke of the effectiveness of Barrus homilies, most of which were five to seven minutes long. "He could say more in five minutes than I could say in twenty-five. Sometimes he would talk for two minutes and sit down—a profound two minutes, each word carrying its own weight," said Father Henry. A few folks still remember with great delight a two word homily he once gave at this parish church: *"Love everyone."*

Although never a classroom student of Paul Barrus, a young parishioner, Nanci Carroll, immediately fell under the sway of his powerful way with words, and they became good friends. Nanci has said of the first homily she heard him give: "I was immediately captivated by both its substance and eloquence. His words nourished and enriched both the mind and soul." Throughout his transfers to other parishes, Nanci Carroll stayed in close touch with him. "We often spoke of our grandmothers and their influence on us. He gave me wonderful advice and became a part of our family." During the last three years of his life, Nanci often visited with him, recording his early Winterset stories and readings of his favorite Bible verses. When her parents, John and Linda Carroll, learned that Paul Barrus had once been the favorite teacher of a woman who had, in turn, become the favorite teacher of Linda, the Carroll family arranged a surprise dinner party for the two who had not seen each other in many years. It was a grand reunion.

On occasion, the Carrolls took Father Paul to hear a favorite Irish tenor in concert. John Carroll also filled another special niche in his life, as he was often the one chosen to spend the night at the rectory in Father Henry's absence, so that the older priest would not be alone at night, especially if he were ailing.

A pattern which had begun to develop while he was still in Commerce played itself out in every parish to which he was assigned. Unable to drive as his eyesight worsened, he depended on others to drive him around. In Commerce, it was Theresa Petter and certain ex-ET colleagues. In Grand Prairie, it was John Carroll and Janie Barnett-Bartosiewicz who most often drove him. Janie had been one of his honor students at ET at the time of Flannery O'Connor's visit and was now one of his parishioners at Immaculate Conception parish. On each of their trips to Commerce, they tried to visit with many of his old friends who soon became her friends, too. She drove him to Commerce for return visits so often that Dr. Fred Tarpley once asked her, when she and Barrus stopped by his house near Commerce to visit, "Mrs. B., what do you do when you aren't driving Father Paul around?"

Janie loved to gather seeds from the roadside on these trips. When she did this, Barrus often asked, "Shouldn't you get permission from the farmer to pick up the seeds?" "Oh, Father Paul," she would respond, "Country girls know they don't have to ask for permission to gather seeds or persimmons!"

In appreciation, he sometimes invited Janie to accompany him to High Tea at Neiman-Marcus in downtown Dallas when he and his Commerce friends met there for a special occasion. For Paul Barrus, whether at lunch in Daisy Sellers Cafeteria in Sulphur Springs, or at a Neiman-Marcus High Tea, a convivial meal with dear friends was transformed by grace into a Eucharist.

Many of the letters Paul Barrus left behind show a keen interest in keeping up with all his friends from wherever he was assigned. In the letters, he speaks of being invited back to ET to attend various functions, such as Homecoming. Long after he had stopped driving, he seemed always to find parishioners happy to drive him to Commerce from Grand Prairie or Richardson for these events which he greatly enjoyed. He also speaks often of the friends who drive up from Commerce to visit him, as he does in this letter to Ralph Wood:

> Once a month Carroll Adams drives to Grand Prairie, and we have luncheon at Neiman-Marcus' Zodiac Room, and Bill Tanner drives often to Grand Prairie to visit me and recently we attended a presentation of "Midsummer Night's Dream" at the Dallas Theatre Center. A few "frills" have been added, but on the whole, it was very well done.
>
> Texas spring has been a little reluctant to appear this year, but at last it has arrived. The bluebonnets have passed their prime, the red roses are blooming along the fences, and the Indian paintbrush brighten the highways. The sunsets have been gorgeous lately, and I'm moved almost to be carried away and use the current inanity, FANTASTIC![11]

While in Grand Prairie, he was still able to travel some with friends. Ralph Wood and his wife, Suzanne, visited his old mentor when possible throughout the years, and he, in turn, visited them when possible in Chicago, Illinois; Winston-Salem, North Carolina; and Florence, Italy. The two men, one a Roman Catholic and one a Protestant, once made a pilgrimage to the shrine of St. Francis in Assisi. They never failed to keep up a lively correspondence. In a letter of July 31, 1986, Barrus tells Wood that he has recently returned home from a Clopton family reunion in Richmond, Virginia:

> I was on the go continually when that Sunday, I awoke early in the morning to labored breathing. Fortunately, my cousin Betty Gibson, and her husband, also there for the family reunion, were staying

next door in the same motel, and they were able to summon immediate help. I was in the Richmond hospital for nine days, and then the Gibsons accompanied me to Dallas before they continued the flight to their own home. I was met at the airport by Father Henry and some of the parishioners.

The doctor said that the damage, if any, was minimal. I am taking it easy for perhaps two weeks more, although I miss keenly the privilege of saying Mass. Last Sunday afternoon, Father Henry set up an altar in the conference room here in the rectory complete with candles, holy vessels, missal and lectionary. What a reviving experience! My "congregation" consisted of two. Father Henry acted as Deacon and read the Gospel; Father Jim did the Scripture readings. I even "preached" a short homily on the gifts of patience and humility that illness brings us. These, I have always maintained, are the hardest virtues to acquire, and, although we mortals resist them steadily, they are the foundations of grace.

This touching line from a Barrus letter to Wood when Father Henry was away on a trip expresses an all-too-human sentiment many experience in the absence of a cherished companion: "The house always seems empty when Father Henry is away."

Barrus always found compatible traveling companions, but one can imagine that these folks must have had trying moments. Cousin Elizabeth Johnson remembers a "quirk" he had about staying in hotels:

Mom (Betty) and Dad frequently traveled with Cuz. Whenever they stayed in a hotel, Cuz would insist that Dad check out his room to see if there was a smell of gas. The windows had to be checked, and he had to be assured the lock on his door was working correctly. He could never figure out how to operate the shower, phone, lamps, etc., and often called them for help. This always annoyed Dad, but Mom urged him to be patient with Cuz.

In a long and very carefully written letter on Castlerosse Hotel stationery, and dated Sunday night, May 15, 1988, he wrote to Father Henry from Killarney, Ireland, where he was traveling with his friend and former student, Dr. Bill Tanner:

> Bill and I attended Mass at the Shannon airport (it was crowded) and afterwards went directly to the hotel. I went immediately to bed and slept five hours. There were various obstacles to sleep on the plane, among them the wailing of children and the antics of three men who had "got at" the Scotch. I was able to offer my service at the hotel check-in as a translator between a Frenchman who was concerned about his luggage and an Irish desk clerk who could not understand him. The matter was settled peaceably.

Just seven pages into a small travel journal he was keeping of this trip, it ends abruptly with the last entry dated May 15, 1988: "It's now 4:35 p.m. and we're settled in a quaint comfortable hotel. The afternoon sun is shining on the sheep grazing on the green hillside as I gaze on one of the beautiful lakes of Killarney."

Bill Tanner picks up the story where the Barrus travel journal ends:

> The following day, we joined other visitors for a bus tour of Ireland. In Donnegal, Father Paul was an enthusiastic participant in all our activities that day, including the climbing of some very challenging steps. We retired for the night to the Mount Errigal Hotel in Letterkenny, intending to rejoin the tour group the following morning when we were all to leave for Dublin. He stayed up late that night saying a Novena, and sometime before morning, he awakened me to say that he was having great difficulty breathing. He was rushed to the hospital and diagnosed with congestive heart failure due to a fluid accumulation in his lungs.

The doctor in attendance told Tanner that his friend would die that day. He, in turn, called Father Henry back in the United States to notify him of this dreadful turn of events and to ask for advice.

Father Henry told him to go ahead with the tour group since there was nothing he could do for Father Paul, and that he (Henry) would be in touch with the hospital to make the necessary arrangements. The tour group had already left, however, by the time Tanner had returned to the hotel which enabled him to remain at the hospital with his friend, awaiting the end. After several days in intensive care, however, Father Paul rallied, and his doctor said he would be able to make the return trip to the United States if accompanied by someone to care for him. Through the help of a priest in Letterkenny, Bill Tanner was able to hire a local parishioner to drive them to the Shannon International Hotel. From there, he made arrangements for their return flight home. As one can imagine, it was not an easy trip. As Tanner describes it: "Although he had recovered sufficiently to fly home, he was very uncomfortable and in pain. Father Paul refused to sleep the night before our flight home and spent the night praying instead of resting. When I went to his room for our departure, I truly wondered if he would be able to make the trip to Texas. Alas, he did."

Although he regained strength after some time, he was not completely well again. Some four years later, Father Henry was once again notified of a transfer. This time it was to St. Paul the Apostle Catholic Church in Richardson, Texas. Because Father Paul was not well, and because both priests hoped he would have a few more productive and satisfying years ahead at a parish he loved dearly, they dreaded the move. Father Henry postponed it as long as possible, but the day came when the bishop said, "Now!" Henry could not bear to leave him behind because Father Paul's fears of being abandoned, of being left alone to die, of going blind were becoming more and more pronounced. When Henry would have to leave for any length of time on parish business, he would say, "Father Paul, I have to leave now," and his friend, feeling sorry for himself, would respond, "I may not be here when you come back." Not taking the bait, Henry would ask, "Where are you going?"

Father Henry convinced the bishop that he had to take Father Paul with him, so they made preparations for their move to Richardson. That Father Paul was happy and loved at Immaculate Conception no one could deny. In this farewell letter to the parishioners there, he reminded them that he had remained behind in Commerce awhile when Father Henry was transferred to their parish:

My prayers that I could join Father Henry had been answered, and so I arrived here on June 15, 1984. The eight years since my coming here have been among the happiest of my life. Perhaps you're tired of hearing me say that Father Henry is like my son, my brother, and my fellow priest, but that's exactly how it is. And you, my friends, are all I could ever have hoped for. Your kindness has never faltered, and I leave you with a lump in my throat. Pray for my efforts at St. Paul the Apostle in Richardson, and do, I pray you, come to see me. You are a part of my life and I will always remember you.

Soon after their transfer to St. Paul the Apostle Church (their third assignment as a team) he wrote to his friend, Ralph Wood:

My grandmother used to say that three moves are worse than a fire. I regretted leaving IC parish in Grand Prairie after eight years with loving, caring parishioners.... As the long years have passed, I've come to see that life is a series of good-byes. I wish our language had an expression like the German "auf wiedersehen."

And then, feelingly, he adds: "God has been very good to me, for many people of my age are unwanted or alone or both. Father Henry and the faithful friends like you are my solace as the shadows lengthen."

Determined to Serve at
St. Paul the Apostle Catholic Church: Richardson

At this point, another very important person came into Father Paul's life. His name is Paul Reittinger, and his parish is St. Paul the Apostle in Richardson. Like Paul Barrus, he was also a native of Iowa, and he, too, had wanted to become a priest when he was a very young man. Instead, he went to war—serving in Korea. He eventually married, had a family, and worked for Collins Radio and Rockwell International until he retired. Also like Paul Barrus, he had lost a close family member to death; in his case, a cherished son. A man who could do things with his hands as well as his mind, Paul Reittinger was very much involved in the church, always doing something around St. Paul's to help out. He remembers well the evening he met Father Paul at a welcoming/get-acquainted dinner for the new priests at the home of St. Paul parishioners: "When I met him that evening, I felt that I had encountered an extraordinary person. Because he was having some difficulty walking at that time, I helped him to his car at the end of the evening, and I knew, deep inside myself, that we would become the best of friends."

Paul Reittinger recalls interesting anecdotes concerning Father Paul's tenure at St. Paul's: "One day as we were making preparations for Mass, he turned to an altar boy, and said, 'Son, are you chewing gum?' And the boy swallowed quickly, and then said, 'No, Father.' Later Father Paul said to me, 'I'll bet he won't chew gum again when he comes up to the altar.' I agreed." Reittinger then continues with another observation:

> Father Paul read everything. He would start every day by reading horoscopes and working crossword puzzles. He would always tell me what was going to happen to me that day. He read the advice columns of Ann Landers and Abigail Van Buren faithfully. He often reminded his friends that those two columnists were sisters from Iowa.

(My perusal of letters in Barrus' personal files reveals that on at least one occasion, he wrote to Ann Landers concerning some advice she had given to a Catholic, advice which he considered unsound. The subject matter of the letter to which Ann Landers was responding was of a rather delicate nature. This may explain why his letter of response to her letter was not mailed.)

About Father Paul's eating habits, Reittinger had this to say:

> He would not eat lettuce or salad of any kind. He would order dessert before he ordered his entrée. Once we were out for breakfast and he ate a hearty meal — biscuits and the whole bit — and then he wanted dessert. The waitress told him, "We don't have desserts for breakfast. There's nothing sweet except cinnamon rolls." "Then, I'll have a cinnamon roll,"

he told her. This after a big breakfast! And he ate it all. When we got back to the car, he said, "Paul, I don't want to go back to that place to eat." And that, after he had told me several times during breakfast that this was a great place to eat. What changed his mind? They didn't have desserts!

He loved chocolates, and he could crunch peanut brittle or hard peppermint candy until you might think he would break his teeth, but he had very good, strong teeth right until the end. He wanted to go to La Madeleine for breakfast so he could speak French with the servers, but so few of them could actually speak French, he usually came away disappointed. Once he filled out a survey assessing the effectiveness of La Madeleine. He wrote his answers in French, and soon received a letter containing a coupon for a loaf of fresh bread and a thank-you note from the manager.

Paul Reittinger (left) with Father Henry and Father Paul

One blistering hot summer day, when he was unable to go outside, he declared to Paul R.: "In this morning's paper, I read that it was hot enough to fry an egg on the sidewalk. I've read this so many times over the years, I wonder if it could be true. Take this egg and break it on top of your car hood to see if it will fry." Paul R. did as he was requested to do, and in one hour he checked. The egg was fried; he turned it over with a spatula and then brought it into the house to show his friend. The experiment now being over — one well-done egg was consigned to the kitchen waste.

"Paul, you should become a deacon," Barrus told Reittinger one day. "Well, I've thought about it," replied his friend, "but the class studying now is half way through the program." "You can catch up!" Barrus replied, "I'm going to call the person in charge and make an appointment for you to talk to him about entering now." As it turned out, Reittinger was accepted into the next class and became Deacon Paul when his class graduated. To this day, he is still fully occupied as a deacon at St. Paul's.

I am not certain how long Father Paul had been at St. Paul the Apostle Catholic Church when I became re-acquainted with him. This is how that came about. It so happened that I drove past that church in Richardson every day on my way to work. I had not been a practicing Catholic for several years, and although I was aware that he had become a priest after he retired, it had not occurred to me that Paul Barrus might be an associate pastor at a church so near my home.

I was suffering a severe depression which had lasted for months. One day on my way to work I was trying to pray, but I was convinced that if there really was a God, he was not listening to me. Alone in the car, I shouted "Where are you God?" At the moment I drove past St. Paul's on this particular day, a feeling of peace came over me. I recognized that God was with me and in all of my noisy agonizing, I had not heard Him. I stopped the car and went inside the church. Mass was ending and people were walking out as I was walking in. As I settled into a pew, I looked toward the side of the altar and there sat an aged priest in a chair. He was restrained by a sash to keep him in an upright position. "Oh," I said to myself, "It's Dr. Barrus!" I could not believe my eyes, so I asked a lady the name of the priest. She assured me that it was Paul Barrus. At the sight of him after so many years, I was overcome with tears. Finally I was able to make my way to the altar to greet him. "Do you remember me?" I asked. And he, with live microphone still attached to his priestly garments, assured me (and the rest of the people who had not yet exited after the conclusion of the Mass, and who also could hear him quite clearly) that he did indeed remember me. He then invited me to come to visit him at the rectory. I said that I would, but I was slow in following through with my promise.

When he grew stronger, later that same year of 1993, Paul Reittinger brought him to Richland College where I was teaching. He had come that day to hear a guest speaker, one of his former students at ET, Susan Wood, read from her new book of poetry. I saw the two men walk in, and I managed to sit beside them. Again, we had a chance to visit, and Paul Reittinger offered to bring him to speak to one of my classes. Much to my regret even to this day, that never came to pass because I did not follow through. I mention it here only to emphasize the degree of dedication to Paul Barrus which Paul Reittinger was already evidencing.

Finally, I did go to the rectory for a private visit with Father Paul in 1994. He received visitors in his bedroom/study. It was a cold day, and he had the space heater turned on high, a shawl over his shoulders. He offered me chocolates. We munched on them, and we talked about many things. At the end of our visit, I walked away as a new person with renewed appreciation for the faith I had left and a determination to be reconciled with my church. From that day on I never lost touch with him again until his death.

Although his small honors classes at Immaculate Conception had been a success, there was concern at St. Paul's about whether or not he could handle a regular class of more than twenty youngsters. The answer became apparent pretty quickly. Yes! I can vouch for that, having visited his class there when I was on sabbatical from my college to observe excellence in teaching. On the day I visited his class I was absolutely enthralled for the entire hour, swept back to the days I was a student in his class, and I was as mesmerized then as I had been in the beginning. Although by this time I had been a college teacher for about fifteen years, I found myself envying these eighth graders, and yes—still able to learn from this master teacher. For the purposes of my sabbatical study, I visited in both elementary and high schools, both public and private, and I also visited in the classrooms of various disciplines in my own college. Nowhere did I find more pure excellence in teaching than in his classroom at St. Paul's. Because it was difficult for him to walk, he was driven from the rectory to the classroom in a golf cart donated by the parish. Fathers Henry and Paul each contributed $25 to the $50 prize which they awarded to the winner of the "Name the Cart Contest." When Father Paul, the contest judge, came to the entry, "*Paul Bearer,*" he rejected it, but when he came to the "*Mass Transit*" entry, he said, "That's it! We have a winner!" And he looked no further. Today, my only regret concerning that classroom visit is that I did not hitch a ride on "*Mass Transit*" as he and the driver waved goodbye to me as they wheeled out of the parking lot after class to whisk Father Paul back to the rectory.

On the twentieth anniversary of Father Paul's priesthood, a reception was given in his honor at St. Paul's. From Commerce, Grand Prairie, Richardson, and from out-of-state came friends, former parishioners, and former students to express their love and appreciation. All who wished to do so were invited to write in his Memory Book. Many of his friends who could not come to the reception sent letters, which are also a part of the Memory Book. I have chosen a few excerpts because they lend support to what Dr. Tarpley said about his friend, Paul Barrus: "He never let go of a friendship. Somehow, throughout the long years, he managed to stay in touch."

Father Paul and Father Henry, Christmas, 1995

From a long-ago student comes this letter: "My first memories of you are when you came to teach school in Hamilton, Iowa. You were my seventh-grade and eighth-grade teacher. In the morning, you would tell us that sometime during the day you would commit a grammatical error, and the one to catch it would receive extra credit."

Another former student writes, "You were by far the best teacher I ever had at dear Old Drake, back in those hectic pre-WWII years." It was also in one of his classes at Drake writes another couple "... where we fell in love, later married, and never forgot you. The best class we ever had was the backdrop for our romance and marriage."

From Des Moines, Iowa, there is a newsy letter from the granddaughter of one of Barrus' teachers who says her grandmother remembered him as "a very good student, and she always asked to be kept up to date on his whereabouts and what he was doing." Yet another letter from Des Moines — this time from a former classmate: "It has been seventy-nine years since we graduated from Winterset High School, class of 1919. I believe that you and I are the only ones left from our high school graduating class of forty."

Letters from former students who became teachers over a span of many years say essentially the same thing: "I frequently use things I learned from your classes to teach mine," or "I try to show the same compassion and concern for my students that you always showed us," or "One English class with you taught me more about teaching than all the education classes I ever took."

Perhaps most touching of all the "Memory Book" tributes he received on that day was this one from Father Henry:

> One of the greatest gifts you have is the ability to see great potential in a person and to encourage that person to actualize his/her abilities and possibilities. And as a priest you are a sign and witness to the divine presence in this world that cries out for redemption. You are an inspiration and hope to those in need of the healing love of God. I am proud to be your "son," your "brother" and your friend. Thank you for sharing your life with me. May God give us much more time together.

Soon after the anniversary celebration which had prompted the letters above, Father Henry was asked by the bishop to transfer to another parish, St. Elizabeth Ann Seton in Plano. No move had been easy for them, but this would prove to be the most difficult of all. Father Paul's health was declining steadily, and his fear of being left alone to die was growing at an equal pace. At the new parish, Father Henry would be shepherding a much larger and still-growing church. His responsibilities there would leave scarce time for tending an invalid, and yet leaving Father Paul behind was out of the question.

He delayed the move until finally, in obedience, he agreed, once again on the condition that Father Paul could go with him. In 1997, with heavy hearts, they both moved to the rectory in Plano. Father Paul was ninety-five years old.

Giving to the End at St. Elizabeth Ann Seton: Plano

Plano, just north of Richardson and about a half-hour's drive from St. Paul's, had been a very small town for many years. By the time Father Paul arrived there, it had become a large city, and St. Elizabeth Ann Seton, although relatively new, had become a large parish. Once settled at Seton, Father Paul wanted to say Mass, but he came close to falling once or twice at the altar, and the parishioners became concerned for his safety. Father Henry decided they should concelebrate the Mass, and that worked for Father Paul, but doubled the work for Henry. Once, while they were both at the altar, Father Paul, holding on to keep from falling, whispered to Henry—whispered, yes, but into his microphone, which allowed everyone in the congregation to hear him—"My pants are falling down."

Soon after this incident and some other difficulties, Father Henry made the decision that Father Paul would say Mass at the rectory, rather than in the sanctuary of the church, as long as he was able to do so. This pleased him very much because it meant he could still be useful. This decision was what led to Father Paul's Friday noon Masses around the dining table in the rectory at St. Elizabeth Ann Seton. When he could no longer go to the people, they came to him for Mass and for small classes. I was fortunate to attend several of these Friday Masses, and count my opportunity to do so among life's special blessings. There was a feeling of stillness, of oneness, of closeness in the room—the feeling that one gets when in the presence of true holiness. It was easy to imagine, on these Fridays when we were often no more than twelve in number, and seated around the dining table, that this was how the early Christians met to worship.

Sometimes the room was filled with twenty to thirty people, but this feeling of intimacy was never lost. More than seven years have passed since we gathered for those Masses, yet the participants remember those special times with remarkable clarity. I asked some of the parishioners who attended these Masses what they remembered as being so special, and to a person, they said that it was the presence of Father Paul, and that this one hour was the highlight of their week.

I was also able to attend some of his adult Flannery O'Connor classes which he taught in the same dining room at the rectory at noon on Wednesdays. For me, this was an absolute delight—a second chance to learn from a master teacher. Here he was, ninety-six years old, and from his wheelchair, leading a lively discussion on an O'Connor short story, "The Enduring Chill." Some in the class admitted they did not understand the motive of the main character, or the meaning of his search, but gradually, through questions and discussion, he led the class to see the man as a spiritually disturbed character in search of a sense of meaning for his life. As a "homework assignment," he told the class, "Before you go to bed tonight, ask yourselves this question, 'Have I ever felt the chill that this man feels? Have I felt the warmth of the Holy Spirit replace that chill?'" Ahh, I thought, the Barrus I remember, guiding students to take something they learn from literature and to apply it to their own lives.

Father Henry had this to say about the O'Conner class: "His teaching and the Mass keep him going. But he wishes he could do more. He wants to do his share. I tell him, 'You touch the lives of people. You give them something they otherwise wouldn't get. You give them both affirmation and challenge.'" As a member of that class, I can say, Yes, that's true. And it is no small gift. It's something that an afternoon of bridge or a shopping spree can't provide. In particular, I remember one writing assignment he gave at this time. It wasn't to be graded but to be read aloud to share with the class. I can still see the twinkle and sparkle in his eyes as I looked up from reading my paper. In that moment, I realized something that I had not given much thought to before—we, his class members, really were giving him a reason for being. Some of the same folks in this small class were also able to take his occasional vocabulary building and grammar courses. I was not able to do that, but those who did so assure me that it was a memorable experience. Class member Cyrilla Wyatt expressed it this way: "I always thought I was a hopeless case when it came to learning grammar. He showed me that was not so. Once I stopped being afraid of it, I learned. Had I realized this earlier, I would have majored in English, which was what I had wanted to do when I was young and went to college."

He had a steady flow of visitors to his apartment in the rectory. A small group met with him regularly to say the Rosary. Some folks came for Confession (now called Reconciliation) while others might simply want to chat, and his telephone rang often. He was not alone.

&

PART V

THE LAST DAYS

Does the road wind uphill all the way?
Yes, to the very end.
Will the day's journey take the whole long day?
From morn to night, my friend.

But is there for the night a resting-place?
A roof for when the slow dark hours begin.
May not the darkness hide it from my face?
You cannot miss that inn.

(from "Uphill" by Christina Rosseti, verses 1 & 2)

Embraced in a Circle of Love

FOR THE LAST SIX MONTHS OF HIS LIFE at St. Elizabeth Ann Seton
Catholic Church, Paul Barrus was physically unable to go into the
dining room of the rectory for the Mass or his classes. He eventually
had to be moved by hydraulic lift from his bed to an easy chair. His
loyal following did not abandon him. Some of them followed him
right into his sitting room/bedroom, where, for awhile, informal ses-
sions continued around the fireplace when he felt up to it. Gradually,
he became more of a participant than a leader.

It was around this time that I learned we had something special in
common. We were both converts to Catholicism. I thought it strange

that I had not heard him speak of his conversion before. Later, in the process of gathering information about him for this book, I learned that most of his closest friends had assumed that he was a "cradle Catholic." I decided that it was probably out of respect for his friends, many of whom were of other faiths, or of no faith, that he did not mention it.

The severity of his health problems at this stage of his life caused many to marvel at his determination to hold on. "He does not want to let go of this world, especially with respect to the friends he has here," Father Henry said, "but he is a man of prayer. Even when he begins to get pessimistic, he takes time every day to say he loves me. One thing about Father Paul is that he respects the relationships he has with the people he knows."

As the year 1999 wound down, and the new century drew closer, his dependence on Father Henry grew mightily. And it was not only the concern for his friend's physical welfare that weighed heavily on Henry, but fear for his emotional health as well. The invalid Barrus grew even more concerned that he would be abandoned to die alone, despite Henry's assurances that this would not happen. Father Paul's need for constant reassurance became child-like, and Father Henry's management of the affairs of a large parish while he cared for his ailing friend was a constant source of wonder to the people who knew them both.

In the light of what William Styron says about his own experiences with severe depression in *Darkness Visible*, this sense of loss and fear of abandonment on the part of Father Paul is characteristic of the disease as Styron describes it: "There is an acute fear of abandonment. Being alone in the house, even for a moment, caused me exquisite panic and trepidation." He explained that he could not have dealt with the disease at all without the constant support of his wife, who became his confidante — "a counselor of rocklike certainty to my existence." He said, "I would hazard the opinion that many disastrous sequels to depression might be averted if the victims received support such as she gave me."

Father Henry had been Father Paul's confidante for many years—his own "counselor of rocklike certainty to his existence"—just the right support he needed for the long haul. Yet, Father Henry knows that he is no saint. Like other poor mortals, he, too, has limits of endurance. Father Paul's constant need for reassurance that he would not be abandoned to die alone, his jealousy when Henry continued to spend time with his other friends, and his ever-growing child-like need for attention wore on Father Henry's nerves, even as he sympathized with his ailing friend. There were plenty of times, Father Henry admitted, when he lost his patience and raised his voice. They never gave up on each other, though. Father Henry says Father Paul was always quick to offer heartfelt apology when he recognized he had been too demanding.

Father Henry would be the first to say the last months would have been impossible without the help and devotion of Deacon Paul Reittinger. Almost four years before his death, Father Paul had written a letter to Father Henry, who was away on vacation at the time, in which he said, "I have never had better friends than Paul and Therese Reittinger. Paul and I know to the last detail the particulars of our routine, and he anticipates the requirements of every situation. As an added benefit, we 'talk Iowa' again and again."

It was almost as if Barrus knew then that Paul Reittinger would still be concerned with his well-being until the very end of his life. True to his undertaking, Reittinger would drive to Plano each night to give Father Paul his medicine and help him prepare for bed before he returned to his own home and his remarkably understanding wife in Richardson. When Father Henry had to be absent for a few days, this devoted man would stay all night with the aged priest who slept with a baby monitor by his bed. From upstairs where he slept, Reittinger could hear when he called out—sometimes two, three, or more times a night. "I would go down to his room," this devoted caretaker says, "and ask him, 'What's wrong, Father Paul?' Sometimes it was nothing more than his wanting to be assured he was not alone."

Father Henry said of this same monitor, "It is not selective, you know. Often during the night, I could hear him calling, 'Father, help me! Father, help me!'" Rousing himself from sleep, Father Henry would have to calculate the seriousness and immediacy of the plea. Was Father Paul in need of assistance this minute, or, was it a prayer? Or, was it a plea for yet another reassurance that he was not alone?

In his last year, while in control of his mind but struggling to hold on to his dignity in cognizance of his failing body, Father Paul often said, according to those closest to him: "Is it worse to lose the mind, or to lose the body first?" He sometimes lashed out at close friends who were being kind to him which doesn't seem to be a characteristic of depression so much as a tiredness which is not surprising for someone of his age. As an example of this irascible turn, two amusing stories from two good friends emerged after his death. In a letter to Father Henry, Marty Manteuffil, a former parishioner from St. Paul's, says, in part,

> Back in September or October, I visited Father Paul while he was in the hospital. After visiting for two hours, I told him goodbye and left. As I was walking down the hall, I heard him yell, "Come back, now!" I returned to his room and asked what was wrong. He told me that he wanted me to rearrange his room. I explained that I could not move certain items where he wanted because it would prevent the nurses from being able to get to him in an emergency. I had never seen Father Paul angry until then. He got mad at me, and told me if I would not move the things, I could leave. I made a point of making up before I left, and I'm thankful I did because I can look back on that now and smile.

Cyrilla Wyatt, a St. Elizabeth Ann Seton parishioner, told of the time she became the target of his anger when she had fussed at him for eating so many sweets. "Father Paul," she said to him, "You eat far too many sweets! They are not good for you. Stop it!" Being ninety-seven years old, and having already consumed enough peanut brittle and white cake with chocolate icing to trigger a diabetic coma (had he been susceptible to such), he did not take kindly to this advice, telling her, "You're a mean woman." Cyrilla stopped visiting her sick friend for awhile, but like Mrs. Manteuffil, she, too, made up with him before long. Cyrilla was one of his daily visitors the last few weeks of his life.

An instance of his exaggerated age sensitivity can be seen in this anecdote related by Paul Reittinger:

> Father Paul was already in his nineties when one day he became very ill. I drove him to the emergency room of the local hospital, and of course, the admittance

nurse asked him, "How old are you?" He refused to tell her, saying without so much as a smile, "You don't need to know that." She went on to other questions, and finally she said, "Your year of birth, please." He then told her the day, month, and year he was born without seeming to be bothered by the fact that he had just told her how old he was.

Paul Reittinger and Father Henry were the most gentle and caring of nurses. Often, caring for Father Paul involved changing his sheets and bed-clothing in the middle of the night with all the effort and patience which such a task entails. Caring for him required enormous good will and endless time. Toward the end, professional nurses were hired to help take care of him. They, too, became very close to Father Paul, a man who was indeed fortunate to have such friends as Paul Reittinger, Henry Petter, and the very devoted as well as the very devout Maria Rudnik, his most loyal daytime caretaker the last year of his life.

"Maria, My Mother Sent You to Me!"

On the day I met with Maria Rudnik to interview her for this story, July 28, 2005, some five years after the death of Paul Barrus, she welcomed me into a sitting room of the rectory at St. Elizabeth Ann Seton, Father Paul's former bedroom where he had been confined for a time near the end of his life. With her rosary in one hand and a journal in which she had recorded her memories of Father Paul's last days on earth, she suggested that we recite The Lord's Prayer before we began our talk.

Maria recalled the day she first visited with him shortly after he and Father Henry had arrived at Seton,

> As we talked, a feeling of great peace came over me. I felt no urgency to go anywhere or do anything after we talked. We sat in silence, and finally he said, "Most people come, and they get up and leave after awhile. You stay." "I feel at ease here," I told him. We sat awhile longer, and then he asked me to call his cook who had not shown up to make his

breakfast. The cook could not come that day, so I made breakfast for him."

After some time, Maria became his part-time caregiver. "On Saturday mornings, Father Paul and I would have a picnic in his room. We always had crackers, cheese, and grapes. I would peel the grapes for him. He would always ask for chocolate-chip cookies. Every morning we said the rosary together after breakfast. One day he told me, *'Maria, my mother sent you to me.'*"

"On that last Thanksgiving day, 1999, I heard him calling me, but I couldn't stop what I was doing in the kitchen at that moment. Then I heard him yelling, loudly, 'Maria, are you there?' I came in a hurry to his room. 'Why didn't you come when I called you? You are not a real Christian if you don't come when I call,' he said to me. I sat down. I said, 'Father, I love you.' He turned his head away."

When I expressed concern that she was treated unkindly, Maria responded, "It was not Father Paul who yelled at me. It was his suffering. He always prayed, 'Jesus help me. Lord, help me.' The gift of taking care of Father Paul was a blessing to me. He told me, *'Maria, when I die, I want you to be beside me, holding my hand.'*"

This request, which Maria immediately agreed to, presented a problem for her since she had to return to her own home in the evening, and if he died sometime during the night, she would not

Maria Rudnik, Paul's devoted caretaker, 1999

be able to carry out her promise to him. "So," she said, "I talked to God, and made a deal with Him." But what was the deal? I did not ask, but I assumed that in her "talk with God," she had promised that if Father Paul was spared from a late-night death, she would be by his side during his final hour. (He had often said, toward the end of 1999, that he wanted to live to see the new century.)

Maria picks up with her story of that last day of his life, January 1, 2000:

> He had visitors in the afternoon. Paul and Therese Reittinger were the last visitors that day. I told Father to bless Deacon Paul and his wife. They knelt, and he blessed them from his bed before they left to go home. I stayed on. Father Henry walked in and out of the room silently as if he were lost in prayer. I sat on the side of Father Paul's bed feeding him ice chips from a spoon. I wiped his face with a soft warm cloth. I sang for him and held his hand. Then, after awhile, he reached upward and took his last breath. With a shock, I saw that he was gone. Suddenly I felt great fear, and then I started to cry. Father Henry rushed in. He said to me, "Settle down, Maria!" And then he started to call, in order, everyone who had to be notified: the doctor, the nurse, and so on.

Paul Reittinger remembers that he and his wife had just arrived home after their final visit with Father Paul when the telephone rang. It was Father Henry with the sad news that the long vigil had come to an end.

Vigil Service and Mass of Christian Burial

The funeral, well-planned by Father Henry, was proper, dignified, and formal, with just the right touch of lightness and humor, the combination that Paul Barrus embodied in life. A twenty-four-hour Vigil Service preceded the Mass of Christian Burial. Friends were invited to bring remembrances of Father Paul's life to the foyer of the church, St. Elizabeth Ann Seton. These remembrances included photos, poems, and anecdotes. Together, they told the story of a great faith hued from a long life of sorrows and joys; a long life well lived. At the Vigil Service and at the Mass, former students and teachers, parishioners, fellow priests, friends, and members of his own family paid tribute to him. At the Vigil, Dr. Ralph Wood praised his old professor for "his virtues as scholar, teacher, and friend," but reached deeper "to salute the Christian faith which was their source." In part, Wood said:

> Father Paul's faith was of the kind described in Hebrews 7 as consisting in godly fear and suffering obedience. It was a faith hammered out on the anvil of woe, and thus it had the strength of finely wrought metal. We would dishonor the memory of Father Paul if we did not confess that his Christianity was deeply linked to his sorrow—a sorrow which began with the death of his young mother.
>
> Yet such grief and sorrows enabled Paul Barrus to become both a deeper Christian and a better teacher of literature than if he had passed through life unscathed. Unlike certain dilettantes within the academy and certain easy believers within the church, he knew that any faith worthy of our embrace, like any art worthy of our interest, must deal with suffering and fear.

In his beautiful eulogy, Dr. Wood concludes:

> The faith of Paul Barrus was the real thing and not a tawdry substitute.... His life was full and true. He believed in the God of Jesus Christ strongly enough to fear Him, to wrestle with Him, to doubt Him. Paul Barrus was a believer, a man who trusted and obeyed. Dread and doubt, pain and death could not defeat him, for he was faithful to the end, a man of godly fear and suffering obedience.

Nanci Carroll also spoke at the Vigil, as well as the funeral Mass. What she had to say is a good reflection of how Paul Barrus transcended barriers of faith, of generation, of all sorts of persuasions that separate so many, to become lifelong friends with a great number of people. She said, in part:

He was most prolific in the language of the human heart. Some people might question how a person of my age could have a deep friendship with someone of Father Paul's age. How thankful I am that he did not define individuals by their physical ages. As I thought about this quality, I recalled a passage that he wrote for the church bulletin at Immaculate Conception around 1987. I have carried this passage in the pocket of my purse ever since it was published. Little did I know that its sentiments would foreshadow my feeling for him now. In it, he wrote:

"Friendship is a kinship of souls unlike physical attraction or superficial appearances. Real friends have a communion of spirit....When he or she is absent, our experience is diminished. When he or she is present, completeness fills our consciousness. When he or she leaves this world, a part of us goes with him or her." A part of me has gone with Father Paul, but a part of him will always remain in my heart and, as he would say, in "memory's album."

In his eulogy, Father Henry moved the congregation to laughter when he told the following story. He had been asleep in his bedroom upstairs in the rectory when he was awakened by Father Paul's voice coming from the baby monitor: *"Come, help me! Help me!"* "I went downstairs, dreading the worst," Henry recalled, "and Father Paul said, 'Would you look up the meaning of this word for me?' I looked at my watch. 'Why are you calling me in the middle of the night to look up the meaning of a word? It's three am.' Father Paul replied, 'Since you're down here already, you might as well look it up'." This story says so much, not only about their relationship but about Paul Barrus as a lover of words and brings to mind once again how Ezra Pound defined *logopoeia*: *"The dance of the intellect among words."* And how could a Barrus student forget what Mark Twain once said: "The difference between the right word and the *almost* right word is the difference between lightning and the lightning bug." Until the very end, Paul Barrus cared enough about words to get them right. For me, and I suspect for many others who sat in the sanctuary that day, the most touching part of this farewell was Father Henry's solo harmonica rendition of "Amazing Grace," Father Paul's favorite hymn.

Cards and letters from Iowa, California, and of course, Texas, arrived at the rectory after his death. They came from all directions, from young and old, with one message: Father Paul would be missed. The most touching letter came from Ken Struble of Richardson, who wrote to Father Henry:

> Your love and caring for him is the most unique story I have ever known. Not only did you perform your priestly duties, but took on this additional physical and spiritual responsibility in such a manner that it stands as your legacy and a tangible example of what Jesus said we should do — love one another. You need never deliver another homily as far as I am concerned, because, by your dedicated action, you have delivered an everlasting one — one without words. No words are needed to explain what is clear to the eye and the heart.

Standing next to Deacon Paul Reittinger at the graveside service in Winterset, Iowa, Father Henry plays Amazing Grace *on his harmonica.*

Amen. All that quiet selflessness through the years had not gone unnoticed. For Father Paul's devoted friend, Deacon Paul Reittinger, much the same could be, and was, said. Others who know both men well consider them to be great examples of how Christians should live. They consider themselves more fortunate than self-sacrificing, having learned and grown and gained from their long association with Father Paul.

Life Journey Completed: Winterset Return

Shall I meet other wayfarers at night?
Those who have gone before.
Then must I knock, or call when just in sight?
They will not keep you waiting at that door.
Shall I find comfort, travel-sore and weak?
Of labour you shall find the sum.
Will there be beds for me and all who seek?
Yea, beds for all who come.

(from "Uphill" by Christina Rosseti, verses 3 & 4)

It is entirely fitting and proper that the body of Paul Wells Barrus, accompanied by his two best friends, Father Henry and Deacon Paul, was flown home to his native Winterset for burial on Tuesday, January 11, 2000, in a place well-known to him from the days of his boyhood visits with his grandmother to the Winterset Cemetery. There he was laid to rest beside his mother, Daisy, and his grandparents, in the company of their many relatives and friends.

Snow covered the ground, the trees were barren of leaves, and even the famous covered bridges of Madison County seemed to hunker down for protection from the cold while the small group — fifteen to twenty or so — sat, huddled in their wraps, near the casket under the tent as Father Henry and Deacon Paul recited the final prayers. As a last farewell salute, Father Henry took his harmonica from his pocket and played *"Amazing Grace."*

EPILOGUE

Our modern era seems to follow the dismal sequences of ancient Greek tragedies: arrogance, over-reaching, indifference to wise counsel. It is reassuring to account for a life well-lived where service to others was elevated to a high art, where ego was restricted to a classroom performance to convey a literary concept and, at its end, a life of scholarship transformed into a life of humble servitude. It was servitude, combined in a magical way through his priesthood, that conveyed to his friends, young and old, a vision of his own good life — to enable better, deeper lives for all of them.

One thing more should be noted. The concept of grace is central to the Christian faith; it is variously and sometimes tediously discussed by learned theologians, but the grace of Paul Wells Barrus was a familiar and everyday occurrence. He found grace in every aspect of his life. His family, colleagues, friends, and students were, to him, the best evidence that the Creator had conferred grace, unasked for, upon him. He found it in the moments of literature, and he took such delights in conveying this grace to his students. Sharing food with those he esteemed at Daisy Sellers Cafeteria or at Neiman Marcus was transformed by grace into a Eucharist. The story of Paul Barrus has come to an end, yet he lives on in the minds and hearts of those who shared his life.

❧

FOOTNOTES
(As Noted in Body of Text)

Barrus, Paul Wells

[1]"A Moment of Grace" columns in *The Commerce Journal*: 1992 and 1993 (See Linck entry below for *The Commerce Journal* reprints consulted.)

[2]"A Yankee Comes to Texas" (apparently unpublished; now housed in Barrus Archives, Special Collections, Gee Library, TAMU-Commerce)

[3]*Levels of Consciousness*. ETSU, Commerce: 1985 This is the first of three small books in a series designed to honor Dr. Barrus after his retirement, and to help raise money for the scholarship fund established in his name at Texas A&M-Commerce. This particular book is composed of two parts: "Fragments of Experience" (which consists of reprinted short stories by Barrus, first published by the English Department of New Mexico Jr. College) and "Teacher from Winterset," a Frances Neidhardt/Paul Barrus interview.

[4]*Visions and Voices*. ETSU, Commerce: 1986. The second book in the series described above is comprised of poems by others honoring Dr. Barrus.

[5]*The Paul Wells Barrus Lectures: 1983–1989*. ETSU, Commerce: 1990. The last book in the series which was begun in 1983 by Dr. Fred Tarpley is composed of lectures given by Barrus' former students to honor him. (I quote extensively from this book, particularly from the essays of Drs. Mark Busby, Ralph Wood, Jerry Flemmons, and Phillip Rutherford.)

Linck, Dr. Charles and Dr. Ernestine:

[6]*Moments of Grace*. Cow Hill Press: Commerce, 1993. Note: It was from this collection of reprints of Barrus' "A Moment of Grace" newspaper columns that I quoted most frequently.

Reynolds, Donald E. and Conrad, James:

[7]*Professor Mayo's College, A History of East Texas State University*, ETSU Press: Commerce, TX, 1990

Styron, William:

[8]*Darkness Visible: A Memoir of Madness*. Random House: NY, 1990.

Special Collections, Gee Library, Texas A&M-Commerce:

[9]Crow, Corrine. Joint interview with Dr. Paul Barrus, Dr. William Jack, and Dr. William Truax.

[10]Rudoff, Judith. Interview with Paul Barrus in 1976. These interviews take place over several days and cover all aspects of Barrus's life.

[11]Barrus and Wood correspondence. Numerous scrapbooks of Barrus memorabilia are also housed here.

Private Collections of Barrus Memorabilia Consulted

[12]Carroll, Nanci: photographs, interviews, notes, stories

[13]Petter, Monsignor Henry: photographs, stories, interviews, memory books

Personal Interviews with Mary Cimarolli

Dr. Carroll Adams, Janie Barnett-Bartosiewicz, John Carroll, Dr. Linda Carroll, Nanci Carroll, Mary Elizabeth Channon, Dr. James Conrad, Dr. Diane Cooper, Dr. James Grimshaw, Cathy Hare, Susie Heflin, Elizabeth Johnson, Tom Johnson, Dr. Charles Linck, Mary Manteufill, Dr. Lawrence McNamee, Ulna McWorter, Annette Milton, Mary Jane Maiers, Michael Nasky, Frances Neidhardt, Msgr. Henry Petter, Theresa Petter, Deacon Paul Reittinger, Maria Rudnik, Vicki Strief, Ken Struble, Dr. William (Bill) Tanner, Dr. Fred Tarpley, Pat Van Hosen, Dr. Ralph Wood, Cyrilla Wyatt

Concerning the Appendix

It has been noted by several people that, in consideration of his reputation as a learned man, an academic, and a skilled writer, Paul Barrus published very little. Knowing him well is to know why. His students were always his first concern, and to them, he dedicated his full energies year after year. A few of his short pieces I have placed in the Appendix to this book. Readers might want to take special notice of "The Furnished Mind," his widely acclaimed 1972 ET commencement address, which I understand was requested by many individuals, one of whom was Felix McKnight, then publisher of *The Dallas Morning News*, and another was this writer who cherishes her copy to this day.

THE APPENDIX

The Furnished Mind
A Commencement Address, May 13, 1972
East Texas State University
Dr. Paul W. Barrus, Professor of English

This is a timely and auspicious occasion. We are subtracting from our days an hour—from the importunate, sometimes impertinent, demands of our crowded days an hour—to grant recognition and to pay homage to man's unique and crowning glory, the achievement of the intellect.

In the words of a famous American, it is altogether fitting and proper that we should do this, for there are manifold forces at work in the world engaged in ruthless warfare against the things of the mind and spirit. Our ears are battered and our eyes sated with the blandishments of sense and the allure of the merely transient. One turns on his radio or television to the caterwauling of an unquiet soul, who, incidentally, is highly remunerated for his wailing and bawling about some visceral emotion that he has labeled love. Encroaching upon the fresh green of our Texas landscape, a billboard hysterically exhorts us to flee from the ostracism that will be surely ours without a sure-fire deodorant to obliterate body odors that have defied the weak potions offered to unsuspecting, unhygienic Americans. From another, a slinky siren with apparently few, if any, inhibitions, models what in less unbuttoned days were known as 'unmentionables.' Still another assures us that sufficient intake of a particular brand of firewater will make us young, robust, sophisticated, and devastatingly 'cool.'

Our newsstands are no mean factors in the mindless catering to raw sensation, though under the genteel guise of 'literature,' their tactics are somewhat less blatant. On magazine covers, however, there is a preoccupation, almost an obsession, with nakedness, which probably is not motivated entirely by devotion to the beauty of the human form. In secluded sections of many bookstores, one may enjoy vicarious orgies without the inconvenience of travel and without the watchful eye of neighbors.

I do not appear before you this evening as a rabid reformer, a nasty prude, or a frustrated pedagogue. It seems to me that any thoughtful person must pause — that he must in all seriousness propound to himself this question: Is this apparent dedication to the cheap, the tawdry, the pathetically temporary an index to the values of our people? This frantic exhibitionism, this pell-mell scramble for the nervous kicks of amusement or the lethal euphoria of drugs, this blind worship of the latest snappy slogan, this scrapping of the lessons of centuries of human experience! Must our yardstick of excellence be 'It turns me on'?

Perhaps the root of our dilemma lies in a philosophy that has unfortunately sprung up with and accompanied the amazing conquest of natural forces which has been the glory — and may be the Nemesis — of our generation. I refer to the philosophy of expediency, the belief that the ends justify the means, though those ends may never have been weighed and evaluated in the light of the experience of the race. Insidiously this pattern of thought has insinuated itself into diverse areas of American life, including that of education.

The problem of the schools has been aggravated by the American dedication to the proposition that a free education is the birthright of all our youth. To this concept we have been committed since the days of the Founding Fathers; it is one of our most cherished ideals. As a result of this conviction, on this evening of 1972 we find our public schools and institutions of higher learning crowded, with new hosts clamoring for entrance. And, mistaking mobs for zeal, size for quality, and palatial appointments for attainment, we complacently assure ourselves that our great nation 'leads the world in education.' Yet we must not be deluded. An educational program is no sounder than the philosophy upon which it is constructed. 'A house builded upon sands cannot stand.' A mighty educational system, however majestic and impressive its façade, is a hollow tomb — a tomb of the intellect — if its procedures and policies are governed primarily by unexamined ends snatched from the flux of the transient and the ephemeral.

You are justified in asking me at this point: What is the unique function of the intellect? And what is the responsibility of the college or university in facilitating its functioning? The fruit of the development of the intellect is a furnished mind and the role of the college is the definition and promulgation of those experiences which will produce that sort of mind. Here ends must be scrutinized for their intrinsic validity; they must not be determined by the loudest advertiser, the most cunning self-seeker or the seductive purveyor of gadgetry.

The criterion for the identification of the intrinsic validity of ends is the extent to which they orient man into this mysterious universe in which, during this brief adventure into consciousness that we call human life, he finds himself. The nature of this orientation — let it never be forgotten — is twofold — adjustment to his physical environ- ment and at-homeness in the world of ideas — pure ideas — to which his God-given intellect alone gives him access. To neglect the first of these is to render man helpless in the face of natural forces; to curtail the second is to make him less than human. It is a deplorable fact that contemporary thinking is centered almost wholly upon the first of these phases of orientation, that is, adjustment to the material world. It has been said that a poll of students would probably reveal that so-called social prestige and success in terms of money are the prime motivators of their matriculation in institutions of higher learning. These goals are not to be held in contempt, but it is a tragic mistake to ascribe to them paramount, if not exclusive, significance. Unaccompanied by the uniquely human and infinitely precious capacity for ideation they are, in the words of St. Paul, become as "sounding brass and a tinkling cymbal."

Members of the graduating classes of East Texas State University, your presence here tonight is a source of inspiration to your teachers, of pride to your parents and friends, and of encouragement to your fellow students. In the days of confusion when men cry 'lo here' and 'lo there' you have not been turned aside from your high purpose. Overcoming the natural indolence that impedes all of us and putting first things first, you have nurtured the flame of intellectual curiosity, which is your peculiarly human heritage. And in so doing you have enriched yourselves for all the days to come.

There is no more poignant human tragedy than to approach maturity with an unfurnished mind, a mind that has no resources in itself, a mind that has depended for its sustenance upon passing fads and physical prowess. When I was a child in a small town, I used to wonder about the rows of older men who sat day after day in the courthouse yard, staring dully into space or whittling, whittling without end. They had come to the evening of life with unfurnished minds. Their lackluster eyes looked out upon a world that was strange, even alien, for the infirmities of age and the decline of passion had divorced them from the only activities they knew. Throughout the long Midwestern summer days, they sat waiting, waiting. Now, when I return home for my vacations, another generation I see in the courthouse yard — still waiting. In contrast with these pathetic figures was an old gentleman named Mr. Cooper. We children at school knew him well, for regularly on Lincoln's birthday he came to tell us a story, the story of Gettysburg, where he, a Federal soldier, watched with a lump in his throat the magnificent charge of Pickett's forces, rightly called the flower of the South, as they swept up the ridge. We always looked for him at the public library, where we scurried after classes, for he was always there. I can see him yet, sitting by the great window that looked out upon Main Street, the light of the low winter sun illuminating his fine old face. We school children involuntarily softened our footsteps and spoke in whispers. The old man was rapt in his reading. He was alive and eternally young in the world of ideas. Throughout the long years he had been busy furnishing his mind.

Barrus Mini-Essays

On Friendship

True friendship is a unique relationship that is developed only with the passage of time. My best friend is my co-worker and companion of twelve years. He is my friend for with him I am always at ease and confident of his uncritical understanding. When I am tired, he restores my initiative and desire to carry on. When I am discouraged, he emphasizes my strengths and minimizes my weaknesses. When I am almost overwhelmed by the perverseness of current trends in society, he renews my hope. He is a constant visitor when I am hospitalized. 'Out of sight, out of mind' is not in his vocabulary. What would I do for him? What would I not do for him? I would never quarrel with him. Perhaps our views vary on certain subjects, but verbalizing them gives them permanence and endows them with more than temporary significance. I can and do rejoice in his presence. He makes me feel secure. I hope I do more than give lip service to the words of Scripture: 'Greater love hath no man than this, that a man lay down his life for his friend.' This is the ultimate test of genuine friendship. Perhaps its implications suggest that we have many pleasant acquaintances but only a few friends.

On the Value of Reading

I am surprised when I find that students don't know the parables of the Bible. I am surprised they don't know the old, old fairy tales, like Grimms. All those things that stir a child's imagination and set him on the path of living in the world of ideas. They lift life above the humdrum, above the zombie stage, into a consciousness of what you are and what you can become. The Bible says where there is no vision the people perish. That's true. Unless we have a perspective or vision of something higher than our daily routine, we do perish. For example, abstract terms like 'forgiveness' and 'love' are hard to define, but if you read the story of the prodigal son, you know what love is. If you read the story of the woman taken in adultery, you know what forgiveness is.

On Suffering

Suffering is part of the inheritance of the human race. Suffering has engaged the best minds that have ever lived. And to me there's no better answer to the mystery of suffering than in the book of Job. He said, as we all say when suffering overtakes us, "Why me?" And the answer, as I recall, was that God asked him, "Were you present when I laid the foundations of the world? Hast thou entered into the springs of the sea?... Hast thou perceived the breadth of the earth?... Canst thou draw out leviathan with a hook?"

On Grace

There is a gift of God that supersedes our acting by blind chance, which uses nature as its foundation, which illuminates human reason, which tempers and directs passion and calms and renovates desire. This is the gift of grace.... Expressed quite simply, it is the supernatural power, based on nature, given us by God, to do what we ought to do. You can tell when you have been an object of grace by the conviction that you have acted in accordance with God's will, with that peace that comes with conquering oneself and aligning oneself with the precepts and example of our Lord.... Grace is always a partner with patience. In periods of silence, we feel one another's wounds, we are a staying presence in times of stress and agony; in other words, we are capable of compassion, a word that literally means 'to suffer with.' The achievement of this involvement and oneness with others is realized only through grace which allows us to stop our mad pace long enough to gain insight into the relationships of those with whom we are associated. Grace can operate anywhere.... How often we poison and destroy other people's lives with a desire to be temporarily prominent and popular by divulging a secret or being the first bearer of a gossipy tidbit. Before we open our mouths with the juicy story, does something whisper, "You shouldn't tell that. It will do harm instead of good."? That whisper is grace working in your soul.... Grace extends into almost all phases of our existence.

The hymn we sing, *Amazing Grace*, is aptly titled. Grace truly is amazing. It may descend upon us without warning when we are sorely tempted; it soothes and encourages those whose hearts are breaking;

it gives hope to the despairing; it engenders that peace that passes understanding.

Excerpts from Father Paul's Letters to Father Henry

Dear Henry, As I listen to your words to those young people, I am thankful for your insight, your example of vital effective priesthood. You cannot know how often you raise my sinking spirits and give me incentive to carry on. Your patience is a healing to those who are used to being brushed off, ignored or made to feel inferior. Your sense of justice is reassuring in these days when self-interest and catering to the wealthy and the powerful result in rationalization of greed, partiality, and mistreatment of the poor, the unattractive, and the miserable. Father Paul

Dear Henry, When I first became acquainted with you during your days in Tyler, somehow I knew that God had chosen you for special service and that He had endowed you with special gifts for bringing the Good News to this weary and confused culture. Then He blessed me in enabling me to share these gifts of yours in our association. Your innate kindness, your sensitivity to the needs and sufferings of others, your tenderness toward those who have wandered away into error, your sense of justice, and your devotion to your vocation brighten the way for all whose lives you touch. Father Paul.

(When Father Henry was away from whichever parish they were assigned to at the time, whether on church business or vacation, Father Paul wrote to him faithfully—sometimes as often as every two or three days. Many of the letters touch on mundane things that are going on in Father Henry's absence, as in the following letter he wrote on July 7, 1996):

Dear Henry,... At five-thirty Mass yesterday evening, the air conditioning stopped, and for a time I was 'hot under the collar.' The temperature was around 105 degrees, and the repairman said that his office had received more than 500 calls for relief. Many of the callers were quite indignant, as if the company they were calling was directly responsible. We are a spoiled, impatient people today. After Mass. the Reittingers and I joined the Snows at Jo Jo's for a bite to eat. Our waitress was Johanna, who provided me with a lemon birthday cake and carried on a conversation with me in German.

Today, Duffy, a visiting priest, and Father Sid celebrated Mass. Sister Dorice called yesterday to say that Father Sid had 'Locked himself out' and hoped Paul R. would 'let him in.' This Paul did at about ten thirty. I see but little of Father Sid, but he seems to be doing well. It was so warm in the church yesterday that I spoke but briefly on one of my favorite passages: Come unto me all ye that are heavy laden and I will give you rest unto your souls. Take my yoke upon you and learn of me, for I am meek and lowly in heart and you shall find rest unto your souls. With hopes of rain and cooler days, Father Paul

From Father Paul's Letters to Dr. Ralph Wood

In a somber observation to his friends, Ralph and Suzanne, he writes on August 7, 1988: In view of the ravages of sin that make ever-increasing inroads on Americans, I wonder how long our nation will continue. I've always heard what Wordsworth calls 'the still, sad music of humanity' but now it seems to have risen to a harsh and blatant cacophony.

By 1992 his letters reveal more of a struggle to remain optimistic in the face of failing health and old age. (He is now ninety years old.) "Each morning when I waken, I say to myself, 'God has given me another day with all its opportunities. Lord, don't let me waste a minute of it in dwelling on my slow walking, my fears for the future, and my un-preparedness in case you should call me today!'"

He rarely talked politics in his letters to Wood, but in August of 1992, he is evidently equally fed up with both Republicans and Democrats, according to what he says in this letter: "I have seen many presidential campaigns, but this one seems to be the nadir of petti-ness, mediocrity, immaturity, and general ineptitude. I don't think our people realize how far and how fast our descent into chaos is. I know that old people are warned not to bask in the 'good old days,' but they were good compared with the mad milieu of today. Oh, for a Jeremiah instead of the 'authorities' who tickle our ears and lull us into a false sense of security."

In a 1995 letter to Wood, he reveals his interest in a young Commerce artist: "For my birthday Dr. Byrd gave me a picture of a Madison

County Covered Bridge. It was done by James Green from a postcard. He is a young black artist of Commerce who has had no formal training in art. His work is truly remarkable, and I wish there were some way it could be recognized." (Nanci Carroll is now the proud owner of the painting to which he refers in this letter to Wood.)

In one letter, he mentions Paul Reittienger is driving him to and fro. This particular day, after the transfer to Richardson, they drove to Grand Prairie to have a former parishioner-dentist fill a cavity for Father Paul, then back to Richardson for a medical check-up, and after that, to a podiatrist who was making an insert for his shoe. The letter ends on a perfect note: "Of such minutiae is much of life composed."

Two Poems by Paul Barrus

Father Paul brought to his students his critical scholarly analysis of poetry—classical, Miltonian and Romantic. His own poetry, as he would have conceded, was of the James Whitcomb Riley variety; carefully didactic, rigidly metrical, and completely intelligible.

Today

The precious days are slipping by.
We do not pause to say
Dear God, how good you are to me.
Oh let us not delay
To thank Him for the breath of life,
The power to lift our hand,
To walk, to talk, to smile, to weep,
Our vision to expand.
Look at the sky of cloudless blue,
The love light in the eyes
Of those who see in us our best,
The good that in us lies.
Teach us to speak in gentle words,
Nor wait until tomorrow
To laugh with those whose day is bright,
To weep with those who sorrow.

"On My Birthday (June 29, 1988)"

I'm looking down the vista of the years
From which emerge beloved faces—
The toil worn hands that wrought for me,
The smiles, the charm, the voices, and graces.
Oh, Father, this I ask of you—
That memory's pages stay thus clear and bright
Until the shadows also fall for me
And to the world I say a last good night.

ↄ